KW-326-301

JACK THE RIPPER

JACK THE RIPPER

A BIBLIOGRAPHY AND REVIEW OF THE LITERATURE

by

Alexander Kelly

FULLY REVISED AND EXPANDED EDITION INCLUDING THE
ORIGINAL INTRODUCTION TO THE MURDERS AND THE THEORIES

by

Colin Wilson

WILTSHIRE LIBRARY & MUSEUM SERVICE

LONDON: ASSOCIATION OF ASSISTANT LIBRARIANS, S.E.D.

1984

Part 1   © Colin Wilson 1972

Parts 2 and 3 © Alexander Garfield Kelly 1972; 1984

Includes items published up to March 1984

Cover illustration derived from *Famous crimes past and present* (1903).

ISBN 0 902248 11 1

Published by The Association of Assistant Librarians, S.E.D.

Printed by
Halstan & Co. Ltd., Amersham, Bucks., England

CONTENTS

1: THE MURDERS AND THE THEORIES

"... Jack the Ripper goes about his business of murder in the elegant overcoat of a member of the Stock Exchange."
Friedrich Bergmann, quoted by Christopher Isherwood in *Prater Violet* (1946).

INTRODUCTION TO THE MURDERS AND THE THEORIES
COLIN WILSON

O N April 10th, 1972, I interviewed Dan Farson and Michael Harrison on Westward Television about the identity of Jack the Ripper; both were about to publish books on the subject. A few days later I received a letter from Mr. A. L. Lee of Torquay, who told me that he believed he knew the Ripper's identity. His father, he said, had worked in the City of London Mortuary in Golden Lane, E.C.1, at the time of the murders. I wrote to ask Mr. Lee the name of his suspect, and he sent me the following:—

"In 1888 Dad was employed by the City of London Corporation at the City Mortuary. Amongst his duties was to collect all bodies of persons who died in the City of London and bring them to the City Mortuary; when an inquest was necessary he prepared them for post mortem by Mr. Spilsbury (father of Sir Bernard Spilsbury). His immediate superior was Dr. Cedric Saunders, the Coroner of the City.

"Dr. Saunders had a very special friend, a Dr. Stanley who used to visit the mortuary once a week. Whenever he saw Dad he always had a few words with him and invariably gave him a cigar.

"One day Dr. Stanley arrived, and passing Dad, said to Dr. Saunders, 'The cows have got my son. I'll get even with them!'

"Very soon afterwards the murders started. Dr. Stanley still visited the mortuary during this time, but as soon as the murders stopped, he was never seen again.

"Dad asked Dr. Saunders whether Dr. Stanley would be coming again. The answer was no. When pressed by Dad, Dr. Saunders said, 'Yes, I believe he was Jack the Ripper'.

"A tailpiece to this. In the early 1920s I read in the *People* one Sunday a paragraph which read, 'A Dr. Stanley, believed to have been Jack the Ripper, has died in South America'."

I must admit that Mr. Lee's letter disappointed me. The Dr. Stanley theory is, in fact, the oldest of the famous theories of the Ripper's identity. It was propounded by Leonard Matters in the first full-length book on the murders *The mystery of Jack the Ripper*, in 1929. Subsequent writers on the case have dealt harshly with Mr Matters and his theory, in fact it would be no exaggeration to say that he is generally dismissed as a liar. In his introduction Matters (an Australian journalist who later became a Labour M.P.) tells how, when he was the editor of an English newspaper in Buenos Aires, he found the 'confessions' of Dr. Stanley in Spanish in a local journal and admits "I cannot vouch for the genuineness of the story". He also says:

"I do not pretend that I shall determine exactly who 'Jack the Ripper' was, but I shall indicate as closely as it may ever be possible for anyone to do so", which makes it sound that he intends 'Dr. Stanley' to be a pseudonym. Many of the writers on the case have so assumed, anyway. According to Matters Dr. Stanley was a Harley Street surgeon, whose son died of syphilis contracted from a rather high class whore, Mary Jeanette Kelly. Mary Kelly's lurid history is given in full. According to Matters Dr. Stanley determined to kill the woman who had destroyed his son; he sought her out in Whitechapel, enquiring as to her whereabouts from other prostitutes, whom he then despatched with his knife to make sure they couldn't warn her. Finally, on November 8th, 1888, he found her in her room at 13 Miller's Court, whereupon he cut her throat and disembowelled her in a spectacular manner. After this he retired to Buenos Aires, where he died a decade or so later.

The story is full of holes. Syphilis could take from ten to twenty years to kill a man, so it is unlikely that Dr. Stanley's son died in two. In any case Mary Kelly was not suffering from anything but alcoholism, according to the coroner. And the story of Dr. Stanley's six-months quest for Mary Kelly fails to hold up. In an area as small as Whitechapel he could have found her within a few hours. If Matters read the story in a Spanish newspaper, why did he not copy it out and quote it verbatim in his book, as any other respectable journalist would do when arguing a theory?

Now if Mr. Lee's story is correct, and he heard it from his father before publication of Leonard Matters's book in 1929, it looks as if we may have done Matters an injustice. The Stanley theory will still not hold water, for a dozen reasons. (No medical skill was shown in the mutilations, the murderer simply knew the position of the vital organs; researchers have been unable to trace any Harley Street surgeon who ceased to practise in 1888 and died in Buenos Aires . . . and so on.) But it *is* probable that a real Dr. Stanley was suspected by Dr. Saunders, as Mr. Lee asserts, and that Matters learned of the Stanley theory from someone who knew Dr. Saunders—perhaps Mr. Lee's father.

So although the Stanley theory remains somewhere near the bottom of the list for plausibility, we now have grounds for believing (a) that there actually was a Dr. Stanley and that Matters was not inventing the name, (b) that Matters's story, although embroidered, is based upon a genuine contemporary theory about the identity of Jack the Ripper.

I mention all this to show that the question of the Ripper's identity is still a matter for active debate, and that fragments of new evidence turn up every day. We are still sixteen years or so from the centenary of the murders, and there must still be dozens of people alive who have their fragment of information to add. I would not be surprised if the question of the identity of Jack the Ripper was finally resolved—beyond all doubt—within my lifetime. Meanwhile we must continue to try to sift out the genuine possibilities from the real absurdities. This bibliography by Mr. Kelly strikes me as an important step in that direction.

Again I can support the point by example. When I was eight or nine years old I read an article in *Tit-bits*, a magazine taken by my grandfather, in which a Commissioner of the Salvation Army stated his belief that Jack the Ripper was a sign writer who had dreamed of blood. One day he told the Commissioner "Carroty Nell will be the next to go". And indeed, a prostitute named Carroty Nell *was* the next to go.

I cited this story in various accounts of the Ripper murders, notably in *An encyclopaedia of murder* and *A casebook of murder*; I also used the idea of a man having "dreams of blood" in my 'Ripper Novel', *Ritual in the dark*. But I had not seen the *Tit-bits* story since I was a child; so in the intervening years I came to believe that the story had been by General Booth, and that Booth was talking about his secretary. Mr. Kelly, with the persistence of a scholar, searched through copies of *Tit-bits* for the late thirties and early forties, and finally came up with the relevant article in the issue of September 23rd, 1939. It was by Commissioner David C. Lamb, not General Booth, and he refers to a sign writer, not his secretary. But my memory had retained, more or less accurately, the phrase "I'll tell you who will be the next one to go, Carroty Nell", although I had recalled the sign writer's "visions of blood" as "dreams of blood". Otherwise the general drift of my version is accurate—testifying to the impression it made on my mind.

The story illustrates two points. First, that fairly unlikely suspects get saddled with the suspicion of being the Ripper. If the sign writer was the Ripper, and if he actually planned on killing Carroty Nell, it is unlikely that he would have told Commissioner Lamb. 'Pre-visions' of violent events are not unusual; Dunne's famous *Experiment with time* contains a few examples, and Osborn's book *The future is now* contains hundreds. Only yesterday a man told me a story of his own clear pre-vision of a room he was about to enter for the first time—a canteen in an old Victorian house. Before he entered the house his knowledge of the room was so detailed that he insisted on stopping, and describing it in detail to his companion (both were builders), before the companion went in and verified every detail. We cannot explain such things, but it is pretty well authenticated that they happen. The sign writer was simply 'psychic'. (Incidentally, Carroty Nell, whose real name was Frances Coles, was killed in February 1891, and most writers on the case feel that she was not a Ripper victim; Michael Harrison, of whom I shall speak in a moment, is an exception.) The second point to note is that I was responsible for propagating my own inaccurate version of this story in the *Encyclopaedia of murder*. Mr. Lee of Torquay could be telling his own story as accurately as he can, and could still be mistaken on important points. The same is true of Leonard Matters and every other writer on the case whose theory is based on contemporary word of mouth.

THE MURDERS

Matters's Stanley theory was, as I have said, the first of the famous theories. Before going on to mention the others I must, for the sake of completeness, speak briefly of the murders themselves. It is unusual for two authors to agree as to which *were* Ripper murders, but there is general agreement that the five crimes committed between August 31st, 1888, and November 9th, 1888, were the work of the same maniac. That is to say, the known Ripper murders took place over a period of a mere ten weeks. These murders were as follows:—

Friday, August 31st: Mary Anne Nicholls, aged 42, known as Polly. Her body was found in Bucks Row (now Durward Street) by a carter on his way to work at 3.20 a.m. Her throat had been cut. A doctor examining the body did not discover

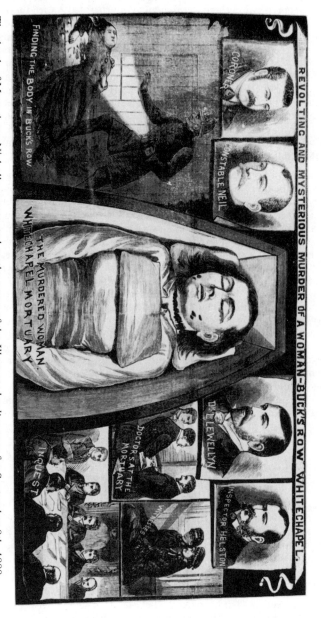

The death of Mary Anne Nicholls as reported on the cover of the *Illustrated police news* for September 8th, 1888.

the injuries beneath the clothes. These were found by a policeman who raised the skirt in the mortuary at the Old Montague Street Workhouse, where she was taken. The Ripper had made several deep cuts in the woman's abdomen, but no organs were actually missing. The murder had taken place between 2.30 a.m., when Polly Nicholls was last seen alive, and 3.15, and the killer had worked silently and quickly— a woman in a bedroom above the murder scene heard nothing.

Saturday, September 8th: Annie Chapman, aged 47, known as 'Dark Annie'. She had been turned away from a lodging house at 2 a.m. and went off in search of a man to provide her with fourpence for a bed. About three hours later she met Jack the Ripper, who went with her into the back yard of 29 Hanbury Street. There he killed her by cutting her throat, after which he mutilated the stomach, and removed a kidney and her ovaries. Two of her front teeth were also missing—as in the case of Polly Nicholls. She was found an hour later by a market worker on his way to work.

The nickname 'Jack the Ripper' was taken from a letter received by the Central News Agency on September 28th, in which the writer declared "I am down on whores, and shan't quit ripping them till I get buckled". The name appeared in the newspapers for the first time on the same day as the news of the next Ripper crimes:

Sunday, September 30th: Elizabeth Stride, aged 45, and Catherine Eddowes, aged 43. Elizabeth Stride, a Swedish woman, was murdered in the backyard of the International Workers Educational Club in Berner Street, off Commercial Road. The Ripper had only had time to cut her throat when a horse and cart drove into the yard; the killer made his escape as the alarmed driver ran in to raise the alarm. At the time of this murder, 1 a.m., Catherine Eddowes, another prostitute, was released from Bishopsgate Police Station, where she had been held for drunkenness. She probably met the Ripper at about 1.30, and went into Mitre Square with him. Her body was found in the corner of the square at 1.45 by a policeman. The throat had been cut and there were several deep gashes on the face; she had been disembowelled, and entrails and the left kidney were missing. Part of a left kidney (either this or another), was sent on October 16th, more than two weeks later, to George Lusk, Chairman of the Whitechapel Vigilance Association, with a Ripper letter.

Friday, November 9th, 1888: Mary Jeannette Kelly, aged 24. This is the only Ripper murder that took place indoors—at 13 Miller's Court, a 'yard' off Dorset Street, now the site of Spitalfields Market. Mary Kelly, an Irishwoman, had a room of her own and had until recently been living with a fish porter. She was in arrears with her rent, and at 2 a.m. had tried to borrow sixpence from a man she knew. A few minutes later, according to this man, she was picked up by a well-dressed stranger who went with her to her room. Neighbours said they heard a cry of "Murder" at about 3.30. At 10.45 the following morning a rent collector looked through the broken window pane of her room, and saw the mutilated remains on the bed. The Ripper had spent at least an hour with the corpse, removing the breasts, heart, kidneys and entrails, apparently working by the light of burning rags in the grate.

These are the five murders generally agreed to be the work of the Ripper. Various writers on the case have suggested that at least five other murders could be added to this total; those of 'Fairy Fay' (name otherwise unknown), December

26th, 1887; Emma Smith, April 3rd, 1888; Martha Turner (or Tabram) August 7th, 1888; Alice McKenzie, July 17th, 1889; and Frances Coles ('Carroty Nell'), February 13th, 1891. There are a number of sound reasons why most writers decline to accept these as Ripper murders; for example, Emma Smith and Frances Coles were both alive when found, although they died shortly after, this hardly sounds like the Ripper. Emma Smith said she was attacked by four men, which seems conclusive. Martha Turner was stabbed 39 times, and several of the wounds were made with a bayonet. Frances Coles and Alice McKenzie both had abdominal injuries, but not to the same extent as in the 1888 murders. It is worth noting that the murders of 'Fairy Fay', Emma Smith and Martha Turner occurred on holidays—Boxing Day, Easter Monday and August Bank Holiday, times when many murders took place in East London.

A few more minor points may be noted. At none of the inquests was there any mention of sexual assault, and it has generally been assumed that *if* the Ripper derived sexual satisfaction from his crime, this was achieved through the act of mutilation. We do not know, of course, whether the doctors who performed the post mortems looked for signs of male semen. But it is interesting to note that Polly Nicholls and Annie Chapman both had teeth missing, while a description of Elizabeth Stride also mentions the absence of teeth in the lower jaw. The same curious feature appeared in the case of the Thames Nude Murders of 1964, in which the six victims were also prostitutes; medical evidence revealed that the killer (who was never caught) had persuaded the girls to perform an act of fellatio; semen was found in the throat of several of the corpses. It is possible that Jack the Ripper and 'Jack the Stripper' shared the same sexual abnormality.

THE THEORIES

The Stanley theory was, as I have mentioned, the first of the famous theories, although some writers might argue that William Le Queux's Pedachenko story deserves precedence. Le Queux was a dubious writer of thrillers of high life, as highly regarded in his time as E. Philips Oppenheim and Sapper. In *Things I know* (1923) he claims to have seen a manuscript (written in French) on famous Russian criminals, which revealed Jack the Ripper to have been a Dr. Alexander Pedachenko, "the greatest and boldest of all Russian criminal lunatics", who was sent to London by the Tsarist secret police in order to embarrass the English police. Le Queux said he found this story in the papers of Rasputin, the 'Russian monk' who was murdered in 1917; they had been found in the cellar of Rasputin's house. In my own biography of Rasputin (1964) I have pointed out the various reasons why this must be untrue. Rasputin could not speak a work of French, as his daughter Maria told me. She also pointed out to me that Rasputin's house had no basement. Nor was he in the least interested in great Russian criminals. On the other hand, Le Queux was fascinated by Rasputin and wrote a wildly mendacious book about him, as well as a novel called *Rasputinism in London*. Donald McCormick revived the Pedachenko theory in his book *The identity of Jack the Ripper* (1959), and still holds to it; in the revised edition of 1970 he takes into account my own objections to the Pedachenko story, but still sticks to his own theory. In fairness to Mr. McCormick, I should add that he also cites a Dr. Thomas Dutton, a friend of Chief Inspector Abberline (who was in charge of the Ripper investigation), who was also convinced that the Ripper was Pedachenko and who sounds more reliable than Le Queux. Dutton's theories are contained in an unpublished manuscript *Chronicles of crime* (three handwritten volumes), and until some enterprising publisher can be persuaded to issue them it is impossible to form an estimate of their merit as evidence.

According to Mr. McCormick, Inspector Abberline also came up with the theory that the Ripper could have been a woman, a midwife. This was later expounded by a writer who calls himself "William Stewart, Artist", in a book in 1939. Stewart points out that Mary Kelly was three months pregnant at the time of her death, and argues that she might well have sent for a midwife; he suggests that this explains the fire in the grate in her room (the blood-stained clothes), and why she managed to escape suspicion—no one would be surprised to see a midwife with bloodstains. The chief objection to this theory is Stewart's suggestion that the midwife then escaped from 13 Miller's Court in Mary Kelly's spare clothes; but Mary Kelly *had* no spare clothes. If she had, she would have pawned them before the murder.

This brings us to the modern theories. There are four strong contenders. The first was the result of a certain amount of detective work on the part of Daniel Farson who, in 1959, compéred a programme on Jack the Ripper, *Farson's guide to the British* (in which I took part). In *Mysteries of police and crime*, Major Arthur Griffiths quotes certain notes by Sir Melville MacNaghten, ex-chief of the C.I.D., in which MacNaghten mentions the three "chief suspects" at the time of the murders. Griffiths omitted the names of the suspects, and it was generally assumed that MacNaghten had destroyed the original papers. Dan Farson tried checking with MacNaghten's daughter, the Dowager Lady Aberconway, and discovered that the notes were still in existence, and the three suspects named as "Mr. J. Druitt, a doctor", "Kosminski, a Polish Jew", and "Michael Ostrog, a mad Russian doctor". (Mr. McCormick is inclined to identify Ostrog with his Pedachenko, and I agree that Sir Melville's manuscript is a point in favour of the theory.)

Dan Farson passed his notes on the case to an American journalist, Tom Cullen, who thereupon did more research of his own on the first suspect, Druitt. Cullen soon traced an item about the death of Druitt (by drowning), in the *County of Middlesex independent* for January 2nd, 1889. He went on to trace Druitt's known career, and produced some of the most convincing arguments so far advanced on the Ripper's identity. Druitt was born in 1857 in Dorset, went to Winchester and Oxford, and looked as though he was destined for a successful career. In 1885 at the age of 27, Druitt was called to the bar. (MacNaghten was mistaken in calling him a doctor.) But that was the beginning and end of his legal career. No clients presented themselves, and after two or three frustrating years, Druitt became a 'crammer' at a Blackheath school. According to the Farson-Cullen theory, Druitt was by this time on the brink of insanity, and committed the five murders, after which he committed suicide by drowning in the Thames. This suicide certainly seems to be the basis of the often-repeated story that the Ripper drowned himself in late 1888. Perhaps the most convincing piece of supporting evidence is that of Mr. Albert Backert, of the Whitechapel Vigilantes, quoted by Dr. T. Dutton. Backert says that in March 1889 he sought an interview with the police and asked what was being done to trap the Ripper, should he strike again. After being sworn to hold his tongue Backert was told that Jack the Ripper was dead; he had been taken out of the Thames two months earlier. That certainly makes it seem that the police themselves were fairly certain that Druitt was the Ripper. Since Cullen's book appeared, Dan Farson has continued to pursue the trail of Montague John Druitt, and promises that his forthcoming book on the Ripper will contain new and conclusive evidence for the Druitt theory.

The solution put forward by Robin Odell in *Jack the Ripper in fact and fiction* (1965) is, to my mind, the least convincing so far. MacNaghten has pointed out (in *Days of my years*) that many of the murders took place in the vicinity of slaughter houses, and that it was widely suspected that the Ripper was a butcher; in fact policemen disguised themselves as slaughtermen to investigate this theory. Mr. Odell argues that the Ripper was a *shochet*, or Jewish ritual slaughterman, the man who prepares 'kosher' meat. It is true that there is a prevalent notion that the Ripper was a Jew; above the body of Catherine Eddowes, someone (probably the Ripper) wrote "The Juwes are the men that will not be blamed for nothing", and Sir Charles Warren, fearful of racial strife, ordered that it should be erased immediately. MacNaghten said that 'Kosminski' was a Polish Jew but there is otherwise no evidence whatever to support Mr. Odell's interesting theory.

In 1960 I wrote a series of articles for the London *Evening standard* under the title *My search for Jack the Ripper*. For when I had first moved to London in 1951 (at the age of 20) I had been engaged on a 'Ripper novel' *Ritual in the dark*, and I spent many afternoons in the British Museum Reading Room and the Colindale Newspaper Library, reading contemporary newspaper accounts of the murders, and also wandering around Whitechapel looking at the remaining murder sites. In *Ritual* (published 1960) I use the actual locations of Ripper murders, but set them in the London of the 1950s. My 'Ripper' is a wealthy homosexual sadist, Austin Nunne. The *Evening standard* articles were timed to correspond roughly with publication of the novel.

I received the usual letters from people with Ripper anecdotes, few of value. (I had already observed that mention of the Ripper seems to touch a vein of free imagination in many people. One old man, near the site of the Mary Kelly murder, told me that he had delivered her morning newspaper until the day of the murder, when he saw a crowd gathered outside, and a policeman told him "She won't be wanting any more papers". When he told me that his age was 65, I worked out that he must have been delivering newspapers at the age of two.) One lady in Ascot told me that her father ran the mental home in which the Ripper died, she did not sign her letter so I was never able to trace her. But one letter from a Dr. T. E. A. Stowell said that I obviously *knew* the identity of the Ripper, and asked me to have lunch at the Athenaeum. Dr. Stowell was apparently a specialist in brain disease. (I somehow got the impression that he was a brain surgeon, and believed this until the other day when Michael Harrison told me that he had checked in the *Medical register*, and Stowell was definitely a 'Dr.', not a 'Mr.'.)

Dr. Stowell's theory was that Jack the Ripper was the Duke of Clarence, grandson of Queen Victoria. He told me he had arrived at this conclusion as a result of seeing the private papers of Sir William Gull, Physician in Ordinary to Queen Victoria. These had been shown to him, he said, in the 1930s, by Gull's daughter, Lady Caroline Acland, a close friend.

To be honest, Dr. Stowell's method of narration was somewhat involved, and he also assumed I knew a great deal more that I did about the royal family. So I am not absolutely clear about many details in his story although he later repeated most of it over the telephone, while I took notes. What he told me, in outline, was this. That Edward, the Duke of Clarence, was a homosexual. That he had not died in the 'flu epidemic of 1892, as the history books state, but of softening of the brain due to syphilis, in a mental home. (When I told him about the lady from Ascot he seemed to feel that this confirmed his suspicion, although on the telephone he told me that Clarence had died in a mental home near Sandringham.) As to the rudimentary medical knowledge shown in the mutilations, Clarence would have picked this up in the hunting field, dissecting venison. When I finally left Stowell after lunch, I was still not clear about exactly what he had seen in Gull's papers. He did not say that Gull identified Clarence with Jack the Ripper, but I gathered that there had been some mysterious mention of the Ripper that led Stowell to reach his own conclusion.

Although Stowell told me he did not want me to publish his theory in case it upset 'her Majesty', he did not otherwise swear me to secrecy, and at various times I told the Clarence story to Dan Farson, Donald McCormick and Nigel Morland. In fact Nigel Morland told me that *he* already believed that Clarence was the Ripper.

When Nigel Morland launched his magazine *The criminologist* he printed a contribution from Stowell on the bones of Edward the Martyr, and in 1970, he persuaded Stowell to write a guarded version of his Ripper theory. *Jack the Ripper—a solution?* appeared in the December 1970 issue of *The criminologist*, and immediately created a furore. Stowell did not name the Duke of Clarence, he referred to him as 'S'. Magnus Linklater of the *Sunday times*, saw the article and rang Donald McCormick to ask him if he knew the identity of Stowell's suspect. McCormick did of course; the consequence was an article in the *Sunday times* under the title *Did Jack the Ripper have royal blood?*

I feel sorry for Stowell, at this stage. I always felt that he *hoped* I would blow the gaff on his Clarence theory; he felt he was sitting on a bombshell and, like a schoolboy, wanted to see it go off. At the same time he undoubtedly *did* have a genuine fear of upsetting the present Queen. So now this theory was out he vacillated. On television in an interview with Kenneth Allsop (whom I had also told about the Clarence theory), he refused to deny or confirm that his suspect was Clarence but allowed Allsop to refer to his suspect as 'Clarence' without contradiction. But in a letter to the *Times* of November 9th he flatly denied that his suspect was Clarence. Startled—and rather overwhelmed—by the wave of publicity that he had caused, he died on November 8th, 1970, and his son destroyed his papers. This of course made no difference since at least a dozen people had known about his theory since 1960. (I told Sir Harold Nicolson about it on the evening of the day I lunched with Stowell; it would be interesting to find out whether he recorded it in his journal.)

But this is not the end of the story. There is an important postscript— so important that it could be the solution of the Ripper mystery.

Michael Harrison, an expert on the Victorian period and the author of many books about it, began work in 1971 on a biography of the Duke of Clarence. Inevitably he had to refer to the Stowell theory so he studied the article in *The criminologist*. What struck him immediately was that the detailed biography of 'S' given by Stowell does not fit the Duke of Clarence, at least not in certain details. But it did fit the Duke's close friend, in fact his lover, J. K. Stephen. Clarence did not die insane in a mental home; Stephen did. Clarence did not resign his army commission at 24; Stephen did. And why, Harrison wondered, did Stowell refer to his suspect as 'S'? Was it because Gull referred to him as 'S'? In that case it seems fairly clear that Stowell jumped to the wrong conclusions from what he read in Gull's papers. He read about homosexual scandals involving the Duke of Clarence (who was apprehended by the police after a raid on a homosexual brothel in Cleveland Street), and dark references to Jack the Ripper which led him to assume that Clarence was the Ripper. It was not Clarence, but the man who had been his tutor and later his boyfriend, Stephen. Stephen's poetry reveals a paranoid hatred of women, and one rhyme refers to a well known poem about Kafoozelum and the death of "ten little whores of Jerusalem". Mr. Harrison believes that Stephen actually killed ten women, the last being 'Carroty Nell', shortly before his final mental collapse. One particularly convincing piece of corroborative evidence is the reference in one of Jack the Ripper's poems (sent to Sir Melville MacNaghten in 1889):

> "I'm not a butcher, I'm not a Yid
> Nor yet a foreign skipper,
> But I'm your own light-hearted friend,
> Yours truly, Jack the Ripper."

Queen Victoria had suggested that the police should check on all foreign skippers coming ashore. This was not public knowledge but Stephen could easily have found it out through the Duke of Clarence.

At the time of writing this introduction I have not had a chance to read the proof of Michael Harrison's book, and so cannot offer any detailed comment on his theory. It sounds, at least, startling and ingenious. Stephen obviously 'fits' to an astonishing degree. (*If* he was finally proved to be the Ripper, it would correspond remarkably closely to my own guess in *Ritual in the dark* that the Ripper was a homosexual sadist with a hatred of women.) It is an astonishing coincidence that Clarence's previous tutor, Dalton, had worked in the same crammers' school in Blackheath as Druitt. Is it possible that Druitt and Stephen had been acquainted, and was this why Druitt was suspected?

What is clear is that here is a Ripper theory that may be proved or disproved by further investigation. This makes it unique among Ripper theories. For ever since Dr. Stanley and Pedachenko-Ostrog, the real problem for Ripperologists (if I may suggest the word) is that it is impossible to 'follow up' the various theories; there is no possible way of determining whether some midwife or *shochet* or mentally deranged doctor was actually the Ripper. Moreover, if, as seems probable, the Ripper was simply a homicidal psychopath, like Peter Kürten the Düsseldorf mass murderer, or Richard Speck the killer of the eight Chicago nurses, then he was a deranged nonentity who has almost certainly left no other record of his existence. As a child I often thought that if some fairy offered me three wishes, the first thing I would ask would be the identity of Jack the Ripper; the thought that it might remain a mystery forever was intolerable. Well, if the Ripper *was* a poet, and a friend of distinguished men, then it would certainly be a marvellous stroke of luck for students of the case; for it would mean that (provided one hit upon the right suspect), there would be a good chance of arriving at some conclusive proof.

If investigation of Michael Harrison's theory proved that J. K. Stephen was Jack the Ripper, then the present bibliography of works on the Ripper would be, I assume, complete and the Ripper file would finally be closed. A sad but exciting day for Ripperologists, and a personal triumph for the compiler of the volume you are now holding in your hand . . .

COLIN WILSON

April 1972.

Part of the cover of the *Illustrated police news* for September 15th, 1888.

MORE THEORIES

The Ripper file closed? Well not quite. Since Colin Wilson wrote those words there have been at least another hundred books and articles published with something to say on the Ripper. If we confine ourselves to new books devoted entirely to the case and to new theories, a few pages will still have to be added to the file.

Renewed support for Montague Druitt as the villain came in Daniel Farson's long-awaited *Jack the Ripper* published just as the first edition of this bibliography went to press. Plenty of circumstantial evidence was put forward but nothing to show that Druitt had been in Whitechapel at any of the requisite times.

Ripper fever reached pandemic proportions in 1973 with the entry of television detectives Barlow and Watt hot on the trail (or rather stone cold on the trail) of *Jack the Ripper* as the BBC series was called. A fair amount of background digging by BBC researchers unearthed two new theories. The murders involved a conspiracy by high-ranking freemasons, including the Metropolitan Police Commissioner. Alternatively, the murders were the work of Sir William Gull, the Royal doctor, and a coachman named John Netley, who chose this somewhat bizarre method of suppressing the news that the heir to the British throne was a Catholic! No explanation was offered as to why Sir William should have departed from the time honoured and much less messy favoured method of medical murderers, who have almost invariably used poison (see Gaute and Odell's *Murder 'whatdunit'*. Harrap 1982.

Donald Rumbelow, a City of London policeman and historian made a determined effort to terminate the Ripper industry in 1975 when *The complete Jack the Ripper* was published. This is easily the best introduction to the crimes and theories but suffered a little through not offering a yet more sensational theory. In his enthusiastic introduction Colin Wilson did his best to fill the gap by offering up Frank Miles, a Victorian artist, as the new candidate.

Richard Whittington-Egan's *A casebook on Jack the Ripper* was somewhat overshadowed by a book which must have some claim to be the most elaborate yet. In compiling *Jack the Ripper: the final solution*, Stephen Knight chose to weave together both of the BBC theories into a splendidly farcical tale. Or perhaps the weaving was carried out by society painter Walter Sickert's son Joseph who furnished most of the 'facts' but promptly retracted his account when the book was published. Certainly it was Knight who 'elevated' Walter Sickert from his position as the original storyteller up to the dizzy heights of co-conspirator.

What can be said about Spiering's *Prince Jack* without being impolite? In this reworking of Stowell's theory the poor Duke of Clarence is credited with enough ingenuity to perform as the Ripper without detection but he apparently had to turn to the literary talents of J. K. Stephen to write the letters for him! After this tour de farce it was a welcome relief to find no fresh offerings in *Will the real Jack the Ripper* by Arthur Douglas; and Bruce Paley's recent article in *True crime monthly* was positively pedestrian in suggesting as the murderer someone who is at least known to have met one of the victims.

And here the case file rests for the moment . . .

"I was in a printing house in hell, and saw the method in which knowledge is transmitted from generation to generation."

William Blake *The marriage of heaven and hell.*

BIBLIOGRAPHY AND REVIEW OF THE LITERATURE:
ALEXANDER KELLY

WHY THE RIPPER?

THE undisputed facts about Jack the Ripper are sparse, even his identity is based on the modus operandi alone and there is no unanimity about the number of murders. Verbatim reports of the discoveries and inquests were carried in several newspapers and much of this information has been reprinted in the books published since. The more lurid papers included all manner of speculation and sensational evidence the like of which has continued to pour forth ever since.

The social and political consequences of the murders began to be explored almost immediately, notably by George Bernard Shaw in the *Star*, and the overall effect of the crimes was to focus attention on East End poverty, prostitution, alien immigration, the inadequacies of the new police force and the neglected field of criminal insanity. Failure to catch the murderer no doubt contributed to the resignation of Sir Charles Warren (the Commissioner of Police) and there is some evidence of anti-Jewish rioting in Whitechapel. The unfortunate decision to erase the 'writing on the wall' is treated fully in several books and is symptomatic of the general confusion and secrecy reinforced by rumour which prevailed. A more recent illustration of this confusion can be found in Woodhall's book which devotes a chapter to a dramatic reconstruction of the interrogation of the Ripper by two eminent worthies (the Home Secretary and Commissioner, no less) and his violent escape and suicide. The whole incident is based on a misreading of five lines from *Days of my years* which served Sir Melville MacNaghten (former Chief of C.I.D.) right for allowing his high-flown style to run away with him!

Why do we still find the Ripper case so fascinating? In the paperback edition of his *Jack the Ripper* Daniel Farson wrote:

"Quite simply, it is a rattling good murder story. The Ripper was never caught, he vanished after the murders as if by magic into the turmoil of the East End, the blood still drying on his hands. His sheer audaciousness seizes the imagination . . . "

Since Daniel Farson also quoted my views on the subject drawn from the first edition of this guide, it may be worth repeating them. I suggested that a major crime only catches our attention if we can identify with the perpetrator. The Whitechapel murders satisfy this need in two ways, by the nature of the crimes themselves and by the failure to catch the killer. Assuming that we are all more or less sexually inhibited and that we suffer some conflict between our moral obligations and natural appetites, it can be argued that we all have a bit of the Ripper in us which makes vicarious indulgence in reading about his activities attractive. The popular theories about his identity (as opposed to Jack the Gorilla or the raving lunatic) all assert that he was more or less normal between killings, thus escaping detection. Various writers have suggested, in classic Jekyll and Hyde manner, that the 'sane' Ripper was unaware that he was also the 'mad murderer'. An otherwise normal individual who in moments of cruelty wrings sadistic delight from his unfortunate victims, seems a perfect screen on which to project fantasies. The idea of the Ripper as a woman (which is usually proposed by men) can also be interpreted in terms of vicarious indulgence, and the view of Jack as a pawn manipulated by devious Czarist agents suggests the Christian role of man as a wicked being acting out a preordained part.

Such suggestions may seem ludicrous, but consider how dull the Whitechapel murders become if committed by a series of different people, by a lunatic with blood-lust, or by a religious fanatic with a divine mission to cleanse the world of harlots. A killer who rationalizes his condition into *believing* that he has a divine purpose immediately becomes more interesting. We might speculate about claims that "the highest in the land" have the same sexual drive as the rest of us, which can be inferred from the jokes prevalent at the time of Queen Victoria's marriage (see Pearsall) or more directly by Stowell's 'revelations'. It is perhaps inevitable that someone with as ambivalent an attitude towards Royalty as Stowell should be a staunch monarchist.

As we move further away from the Ripper in time, the events take on increasingly the character of folklore. The theories become wilder and every statement is countered and refuted. Most of the theories have fairly obvious literary (or at least fictional) antecedents—a quick roll call would take in *The murder in the Rue Morgue* (Jack the gorilla), *Dr Jekyll and Mr Hyde* (Dr Stanley), Conrad's *The secret agent* (Pedachenko) and what about Montague Druitt, the cricket-playing gentleman with a more rewarding after-hours hobby? Raffles take a bow. Even Sir William Gull was preceded into print by ". . . a loyal and chivalrous gentleman" according to Sherlock Holmes in *The illustrious client.* Fortunately we are unlikely to take the master detective's advice to "Let that now and forever be enough for us."

Just as in other forms of folk literature there are signs of the singers taking over from the song. Speculations about the identities and characters of Ripper-writers haven't yet reached the level associated with Homer but the early signs are there. We have already heard of stolen letters, burnt archives, disappearing witnesses and untraceable publications. New theories spill from the lips of television detectives as though to obscure the arm supporting the pointing finger. (With this subtle blending of fact and fantasy is there any wonder that, after Jack himself, New Scotland Yard receives most letters about Sherlock Holmes?) Tireless Ripper hunters pursue their clues into the Australian outback and to a South American deathbed. Now we are told of devious motives amongst the criminous scribes, of witnesses dramatically silenced and writers dying of fear! The identities of these authors fade into the East End fog; even the compiler of this bibliography may not exist.

A DIGRESSION ON EYEBALLS

Most writers of books on the Ripper, from William Stewart (p. 149) onwards, have referred to supposed police attempts to photograph the eyes of various corpses. The idea was to try to retrieve the image of the murderer which was supposed to be retained on the retina after death. Whether or not the police made any such attempt, this superstition was prevalent for some time before and after the murders. In his *Diaries* for April 1701, John Evelyn mentions a Dutch boy with scriptural texts inscribed on his eyeballs. Later R. W. Hackwood, writing in *Notes and queries* (October 1857) quoted a *New York observer* claim that retention of retinal impressions after death was "recently announced in the English papers". He went on to report a *Chicago daily democratic press*   account of successful experiments by Dr. Pollock of Chicago in August 1857 using a microscope and of Dr. Sandford who examined the eyes of J. H. Beardsley (a murder victim) and found a partial image.

Villiers de L'Isle Adam gave new currency to the idea in his story *Claire Lenoir* which was celebrated in *A rebours* (1884) by Huysmans and which in turn was to achieve notoriety as the "yellow-back French novel" featured at the first trial involving Oscar Wilde. This stream of literary borrowings was tapped for the lay public by Geo. R. Richmond of the *New York tribune* who recorded allegations "that an assassin had been convicted in France on the strength of 'eyeball photography'". The *British journal of photography* relayed the Richmond article under the heading *Brain pictures: a photo physiological discovery*, forging a possible link with the police experiment, because the item appeared in early 1888.

Assuming that the police were not avid readers of photography magazines, the French detective Gustave Macé provided an alternative source in his autobiographical *My first crime* published in London in 1886. He recalled receiving a letter claiming that "a celebrated American doctor hit upon the ingenious idea of examining the eyes of a woman who had just been murdered." Although this experiment was pronounced successful, Macé's correspondent was clearly not convinced that it would work again. He included elaborate instructions for replicating the experiment—along with the head of a recently murdered woman to try it out on! Macé was able to catch the villain without resorting to a "magnifying photographic camera" as instructed.

Perhaps Rudyard Kipling was inspired by newspaper reports of the supposed police experiment. In any case he took up the idea in his fine short story *At the end of the passage* which was first published in August 1890. A little later Jules Verne had the victim's son kiss his father's photograph to reveal the assassin's features in the pupils in *Les freres Kip*. According to Marcel Moré, Verne was influenced by an account in La Grange and Valude's standard *Encyclopédie française d'opthalmogie* of some experiments conducted by Giraud-Teulon.

Further incidental references on the murder victim's eyes theme were contributed by James Joyce in *Ulysses* (1922) and by Graham Greene in *The power and the glory* (1940). But in case we should imagine that this idea now belonged entirely to the world of literature, one of the gruesome features of the murder of

P.C. Gutteridge by Browne and Kennedy in 1927 was the apparent attempt to destroy evidence by shooting out both of his eyes.

REFERENCES

British journal of photography (London). February 17th 1888 page 105. Quotes Geo. R. Richmond in the *New York tribune* of January 15th 1888 page 6.

Greene, Graham *The power and the glory* Heinemann (London) 1940. "There was a legend believed by many criminals that dead eyes held the picture of what they had last seen . . ."

Hackwood, R. W. Contribution to *Notes and queries* (London) October 3rd 1857 (Second series vol. IV) page 268.

Joyce, James *Ulysses* Bodley Head (London) 1936. See page 93.

Kipling, Rudyard *At the end of the passage*, a short story in *Lippincott's monthly magazine* (London) August 1890; later collected in *Life's handicap* MacMillan (London) 1891.

Macé, Gustave *My first crime* 307p. Vizetelly (London) 1886. See page 93.

Moré, Marcel *Les tres curieux Jules Verne* Gallimard (Paris) 1960.

Moré, Marcel *Nouvelles explorations de Jules Verne: musique, misogamie, machine* Gallimard (Paris) 1963.

P'u Sung Ling *The talking pupils* in *Strange stories from a Chinese studio* de la Rue (London) 1880. Translator Herbert Giles claimed that "The belief that the human eye contains a tiny being of human shape is universal in China."

Quatro mosche de velluto grigio (1972). An Italian horror film which resurrected the myth.

Verne, Jules *Les freres Kip* (Paris) 1902.

Villiers de L'Isle Adam, Philipe Auguste Mathias *Claire Lenoir* in *Tribulat Bonhommet* Paris 1887; originally published in *Revue des lettres des arts* Paris 1867.

THE CASE OF THE MISSING FILES

Ripper writers have shown great ingenuity in putting the mirkiest possible interpretation on all the information that comes to hand in pursuit of their pet theories. It is hardly surprising then that the same approach has been adopted when information doesn't come to hand. The most extreme example of several occurs in the recent book by Spiering. Faced with the shocking revelation that the official files on the case were incomplete he drew the most sinister inference—an official cover-up!

A few factors suggest that the Spiering conspiracy theory (and other earlier versions) was a little simplistic. Examination of other police files of the same era reveal much the same picture, suggesting that inefficient record keeping, loss in transit round the offices and the confusion brought about by five removals of the entire Metropolitan Police collection to new offices or premises were at least partially responsible for the losses. (Files still occasionally get mislaid at New Scotland Yard even though an elaborate system attempts to keep track of where they are at any time.) The indexing systems employed by the Home Office and the Metropolitan Police in the 1880s were very crude; some Ripper files may be sitting unnoticed elsewhere in these systems. More significantly, the local records for H and J Divisions, which covered Whitechapel and Bethnal Green, have not survived (nor have most other Divisional records of that period) probably because they were not seen as important. Since those records would have included all the local operational information on the case, this is a severe loss to Ripperologists. Only Donald Rumbelow (a serving City of London Policeman) knows the full state of the City Police files on the Ripper.

Some of the Home Office files on the case have indeed been lost or pillaged over the years and 23 out of 298 of the Metropolitan Police files have disappeared (according to William Vincent's figures). Before opting for the conspiracy theory, however, another possibility should be considered. Thousands of people are interested in Jack the Ripper. Scotland Yard receives hundreds of letters every year on the subject. Over the years it is reasonable to assume that a few of these people will have gained access to the official files. Spiering himself describes how he bribed an official to obtain illegal photocopies of a document. In the seventy years or so before photocopiers became readily available someone who wanted a document badly enough would have only one resort—rip it off!

To illustrate the dangers of leaping to conspiracy conclusions, take Spiering's illicitly photocopied report. This came from Inspector Abberline and referred to an 'important statement' from George Hutchinson. After quoting the report Spiering adds "Naturally the important statement he refers to is no longer contained in the file." What could the poor crime researcher do when faced with such a missing link? Well, he could start by checking his facts. The missing statement was still on the file in 1979, a year after Spiering's book was published. But why go to the effort of searching for it when it is quoted in full in Stephen Knight's book published two years earlier and when the first page is used as an illustration?

One other idea which persists in relation to contemporary Ripper records is that they have now been worked over so thoroughly that no fresh information is likely to emerge. Just a single illustration may counter that view and help undermine at least two of the popular theories about the killer's identity.

Both the Druitt and Duke of Clarence theories base part of their argument on the authorities knowing who the Ripper was and that he was drowned or secured by the end of 1888. With this knowledge an obvious step to take would be to call off the hunt (and Spiering claims that the hunt *was* called off). But where is the supporting evidence?

One reason why there was little apparent increase in police presence in Whitechapel in 1888, despite heavy reinforcements from other Divisions, was that over a hundred policemen were put on plain clothes duty. Did they all revert to their old Divisions in November (Clarence theory) or December (Druitt theory)? The short answer is no. Not until five weeks after the last murder (as accepted in both theories) did the first few policemen return to their own Divisions, and the trickle continued over the next few months. More convincing is the fact that over fifty plain clothes police were still being employed on special duty in Whitechapel as late as February 1890, more than a year after Druitt's suicide. Detailed information has survived on police movements at the time but the source is not obvious. I am willing to make all this information available — at the right price!

SELECTION

I have tried to list all important items published in the English language and outstanding foreign works. 'Important' has been interpreted as meaning any new theory, fact or clear re-statement of existing information. The yardstick for fictional material of all kinds has been a clear derivation from the Ripper 'theme' or a significant appearance by the Ripper in a work.

1 CONTEMPORARY RECORDS

All material originally published after 1891 has been excluded from this section which is largely made up of references to newspapers and periodicals of the day. One difficulty arose over the constant repetition of murder reports and inquests which did not differ markedly in style or content whether the vehicle was *The Times, The Star* or a local rival.

Any prize for wringing copy out of the situation would probably go to the *Pall Mall gazette*, an evening paper which made something of a fetish of collecting other people's ideas on the case (mostly from the morning dailies). The *Gazette* records the 'going-rate' for pickled corpses and uses the opportunity of the double murder to attack government policy towards Ireland! (October 1st, 1888). It lists the "suggestions of the public" including "Everyone to report to the police before going to bed," (presumably so that they could more readily be killed on the way home), issuing rubber shoes to policemen who might also be disguised as women, and equipping street-walkers with pistols (October 3rd). Apart from the ideas recorded below, the *Gazette* suggested that the scenes of crime formed a cryptogrammatic dagger, and that the Ripper was an Army doctor suffering from sun stroke who "has seen the horrible play" (*Dr. Jekyll and Mr. Hyde*). The idea of "baby-faced pugilists dressed as women" was championed because "policemen have beards, bass voices, and big feet", which probably represents the nicest thing written about that band of men at the time.

WHITECHAPEL, 1888.

First Member of "Criminal Class." "FINE BODY O' MEN, THE PER-LEECE!"
Second Ditto. "UNCOMMON FINE!—IT'S LUCKY FOR HUS AS THERE'S SECH A BLOOMIN' FEW ON 'EM!!!"

"I have to observe that the Metropolitan Police have not large reserves doing nothing and ready to meet emergencies; but every man has his duty assigned to him, and I can only strengthen the Whitechapel district by drawing men from duty in other parts of the Metropolis."—*Sir Charles Warren's Statement.* "There is one Policeman to every seven hundred persons."—*Vide Recent Statistics.*

A comment on the apparent shortage of police in Whitechapel, published in *Punch*.
(Reproduced by permission of *Punch*).

The audience which gloated over details of the crimes sprang from Aldous Huxley's nineteenth century "Age of innocence — the innocence of those who grind the faces of the poor, but refrain from pinching the bottoms of their neighbours' wives!"

As an exhaustive *Index to the Times* is available for the period I have only noted the titles of newspapers which gave saturation coverage to the murders, together with major articles. The first signs of the Ripper industry were becoming evident at this period both in Britain and America, with the pamphlets by Brewer and Fox. A number of broadsheets were issued to celebrate the latest atrocity but few of these have so far been traced because the large public collections have not been properly indexed. Potential sources for patient researchers in England include the British Museum Library in London and the John Johnson Collection in the Bodleian Library, Oxford.

Arbeter Fraint (London) December 21st 1888. An article by Benjamin Feigenbaum in the weekly journal of this East End radical group, fulminates against religious bodies in general and the *Church times* in particular after a suggestion that the Ripper was a Russian anarchist. (See Fishman, *q.v.* p. 162)

Barker, Richard H. (editor) *The fatal caress and other accounts of English murders from 1551 to 1891* 210 p. Duell, Sloan and Pearce (New York) 1947. The preface by Anthony Boucher succinctly relates some fictional variations of the theme. Barker describes the Ripper as a whimsical fellow and "middle aged professor with a passion for practical jokes". pp. 164-209 carry the *Times* reports of 1888.

Bocock, John Paul Article in the *New York world* (1888) ascribed the murders to Nicolas Vassili, a Russian member of the 'Shorn' sect (according to R. K. Fox).

Brewer, John Francis *The curse upon Mitre Square AD 1530-1888* 72p. Simpkin, Marshall (London) 1888. The return of Brother Martin after three and a half centuries to wreak more vengeance upon womankind.

British journal of photography (London) October 19th 1888 p. 659; 660. Critical of police for failure to use photography at scenes of crime and suggests divisional photographers. Comments on facsimile posters relating to the case.
November 16th 1888 p. 723. Records use of photographs at Kelly murder, reiterates suggestion for divisional photographers.

British medical journal (London) notably the issue for October 6th 1888 pp. 768-9 *The East End murders: detailed lessons*, a moral rather than a medical tract. Denounces its readers for indifference and claims that the police "need to be quickened by a higher sense of public morality".

Commonweal (London) The organ of the Socialist League, edited by William Morris until 1889 when the anarchists gained control.

County of Middlesex independent January 2nd and 5th 1889, reported the death of Cullen's suspect Druitt.

Daily chronicle (London)

Daily news (London) Continuous commentary on the murders and inquests. Theories propounded feature the Ripper in women's clothes, as a Texan or fanatical vivisectionist, as a policeman, and using the sewers as an escape route. See also Archibald Forbes.

Daily telegraph (London) Contemporary issues. That for October 4th 1888 carried a facsimile of a 'Ripper' letter and postcard. Also advocated police right to stop and search people for knives.

East London advertiser

East London observer

Evening news (London)

Evening standard (London)

Forbes, Archibald *The motive of the murders*. Letter to the *Daily news* published on October 3rd 1888 p. 6 labels the killer as a monomaniac seeking "revenge against the class a member of which has wrought him his blighting hurt". Perhaps an "excitable medical student".

Fortnightly review of politics, literature and the arts (London)

(Fox, Richard Kyle) *The history of the Whitechapel murders: a full and authentic narrative of the above murders with sketches* 48 p. Fox (New York) 1888. The editor of the *National police gazette* rehashes news reports of nine murders padded out by a paraphrase of de Quincey's version of the Ratcliffe Highway murders. Attributes crimes to Nicolas Vassili. See John Paul Bocock. (Scarce item available in New York Public Library.)

Fun (London) See also Christopher Pulling.

Ghastly murder in the East End 1888. Broadsheet reproduced in Cullen.

Hansard's parliamentary debates (*Commons*) The record of what is said in the Lower House of Parliament. An index is available for the period but some key items include:

November 14th 1888. Debate on police handling of the case.
July 29th 1889.   Home Secretary refuses to offer a reward.
July 29 1889.   Question about a man charged with assault, then released.
July 3rd 1890.   Question about William Brodie who confessed to White-
                    chapel murder.
July 3rd 1890.   Complaint about crime and vice in Whitechapel.
February 17th to March 9th 1891.   Questions about treatment of Sadler who was
                    charged with murder of Frances Coles.

Hayne, W. J. *Jack the Ripper: or the crimes of London* 1889. Stolen from the Library of Congress and untraced elsewhere.

Illustrated police news law courts and weekly record (London) The issue for August 18th 1888 carried a report and illustration of *Tragedy in Whitechapel. A woman stabbed in thirty-nine places* then from September 8th to December 8th inclusive this sensation sheet kept the murders 'on the boil' with a weekly report, always on page 2, and a total of 184 cover pictures of uniformly crude appearance. Sporadic coverage to 1892.

The issues for September 8th and 22nd, October 6th and 20th, and November 17th 1888 were reproduced in *Great newspapers reprinted 25* February 1974 published by Peter Way Ltd (London). The introduction draws heavily on the first edition of this bibliography.

Jack the Ripper at work again. Another terrible murder and mutilation in Whitechapel 4p. (No publisher given) (November 9th 1888). Broadsheet with pictures of the "Supposed murderer" and "the victim", two columns of news and four of doggerel. In Bodleian Library, John Johnson Collection (Oxford).

Justice (London) Voice of the Social Democrats.

Lancet (London) This medical journal challenged the view that the Ripper was a lunatic (September 15th 1888) and carried a letter from Dr. Henry Sutherland on September 22nd which diagnosed that "he or they are of perfectly sound mind"(!). It commented on Coroner's court evidence (September 29th) and urged sanitary reform in Whitechapel (October 6th).

Moonshine (London)

Morning post (London)

National police gazette (New York) Contemporary issues.

New York daily graphic October 4th 1888 p. 744 *London's ghastly mystery.* Records Dr. J. G. Kiernan's view that the Ripper was a cannibal.

News of the world (London)

North London Press

Ochrana gazette Journal of the Russian secret police quoted by McCormick.

Pall Mall gazette: an evening newspaper and review (London) Plethora of material includes details of murders and inquests and a host of suggestions e.g. bloodhounds, beagles, women detectives, and pugilists in drag; pictures the Ripper as a Malay, Russian, Frenchman or policeman. An index is available. See introduction to this section.

The Penny illustrated paper and illustrated times (London)

The Penny pictorial news (London) Especially September 15th, October 6th and 13th and November 17th 1888.

The People (London)

Police gazette (London) The issue for October 26th 1888 has a series of descriptions of the wanted man.

Pulling, Christopher *Mr. Punch and the police* Butterworths (London) 1964. pp. 120-30 describe reactions to the murders in *Punch* and elsewhere. Reproduces anti-establishment cartoons from *Fun* one of which demands the resignation of the Home Secretary. Remarks on friction between the City and Metropolitan Police.

Punch or the London Charivari (London) See also previous entry.

Reynolds news (London)

Saturday review of politics, literature, science and art (London) for July 20th 1889 pp. 64-65 *The Whitechapel murders.* Argues that "It is therefore natural ... that these crimes should fail to arouse any genuine public interest". Implies that their coverage was caused by a lack of alternative news.

Shaw, George Bernard *Blood money for Whitechapel* a leading article putting the socialist viewpoint in the *Star* of September 24th 1888. Shaw also wrote an unpublished letter to the *Star* as from J. C., abhoring capital punishment and repudiating attempts to catch the murderer. See his *Collected letters 1874-1897* (p. 197) Reinhardt (London) 1965.

Snyder, Louis Leo and Morris, Richard Brandon (editors) *Treasury of great reporting: literature under pressure from the sixteenth century to our time* 784 p Simon and Schuster (New York) 1949. Includes *Times* article by John Williams *I sent you half a kidne . . .*

Southern guardian (Wimbourne, UK) Issue for January 5th 1889 carried inquest report on Cullen's suspect Druitt.

Spectator (London) July 27th 1889 pp. 107-8 *False clues* quotes a *New York herald* article about a sailor suspect and concludes "It is hoped that others ... will act on a less simple and easy assumption than that of hunting for a man who will fit their theories".
March 7th 1891 pp. 335-6 *The Whitechapel murder* suggests that Frances Coles was a Ripper victim and that he would have remained equally undetected in Paris, Vienna or New York.

The Standard (London)

The Star (London) Covers the usual ground including woman and policeman hypotheses. See also George Bernard Shaw.

Sunday times (London)

The Times (London) The index for 1888-9 has a series of relevant entries. See also Barker, Richard (editor); Snyder, L. L. and Morris, R. B. (editors); FACTS and THEORIES: Barnard, Allan (editor).

Two more horrible murders in the East End 1888. Broadsheet reproduced in Cullen.

Warden, Rob and Groves, Martha (editors) *Murder most foul and other great crime stories from the world press* Ohio U.P. (Chicago) 1980. A chapter reprints the *Times* reports on the death of Annie Chapman.

Warren, Charles *Sir Charles Warren defends the force* in *Pall Mall gazette* and the *Daily news* on October 4th 1888. The Commissioner of Police replies to the Whitechapel District Board of Works.

The Whitechapel murders or the mysteries of the East End Nos. 1-5 (incomplete) 40p. Purkess (London) 1888. A strange collection of fact and fantasy preserved in the John Johnson collection of the Bodleian Library. Purkess also owned the *Illustrated police news*.

Most other newspapers and periodicals of the day are worth checking.

2 FACTS AND THEORIES

The books devoted to the Ripper are usually characterized by a painstaking build-up of facts and theories followed by a vertiginous leap into fantasy in the closing chapters. There are now at least eight books available giving access to most of the main facts and theories about the Ripper. The best general guide is Donald Rumbelow's *The complete Jack the Ripper*, but only the hardback edition can be recommended (if you can still find it). Unfortunately the paperback version lacks both Colin Wilson's lively introduction and an index. Both Daniel Farson's *Jack the Ripper* and Stephen Knight's *Jack the Ripper: the final solution* were still available in paperback at the time of writing and are recommended reading; the books by Whittington-Egan and Douglas could also obtained. An 'earlier generation' of books by Odell, Cullen and McCormick still crop up in second-hand bookshops and are worth tracking down.

Theories about the Ripper's identity are legion and range from an escaped orang-outang to the poet Swinburne and from Jill the Ripper to most members of the Royal household. If contemporary police statements were both vague and contradictory, the theorists who followed might perhaps have taken note of the *Spectator* advice to "act on a less simple assumption than that of hunting for a man who will fit their theories". Most of the hypotheses have been recorded in one or other of the books already mentioned but I have attempted to indicate the general approach of each writer below.

Aberconway, Lady Christabel Letter in *New statesman* (London) on November 7th 1959. Lady Aberconway, MacNaghten's daughter, claimed to possess "my father's notes on Jack the Ripper" naming three suspects.

Adam, Hargrave Lee *George Chapman* in *The Black Maria or the criminals omnibus* edited by Harry Hodge. Gollancz (London) 1935. pp. 646-656 reiterate his earlier material. See below.

Adam, Hargrave Lee *Trial of George Chapman* 223 p. Hodge (London) 1930. In *Notable British trials* series. Dismisses the unsupported testimony of MacNaghten, Anderson and Sir Henry Smith who claimed to know the Ripper's identity. Tabulates "the case for supposing" that Chapman was the Ripper. Cites Chief Inspector Abberline in support of the theory but acknowledges that it is inconclusive.

Alexander, Marc *Royal murder* 221p. Muller (London) 1978. Includes a chapter by Colin Wilson on the Ripper outlining the events and the Clarence, Stephen and Gull/Netley theories. "No favourite candidate."

Ambler, Eric *The ability to kill and other pieces* 191p. Bodley Head (London) 1963. Includes nine pages outlining the crimes and the suggestion that "Having achieved an apotheosis of horror, he had at last exorcised the evil that had haunted him."

Anderson, Robert *Criminals and crime: some facts and suggestions* 182 p. Nisbet (London) 1907. The then head of the Criminal Investigation Department makes a passing reference on page five to the Ripper being "safely caged in an asylum".

Anderson, Robert In his preface to *The police encyclopaedia* volume one by Hargrave Lee Adam, 237 p. Routledge (London) 1911, Anderson claimed that "there was no doubt as to the identity of the criminal".

Archer, Fred *Ghost detectives: crime and the psychic world* 176 p. W. H. Allen (London) 1970. Retells the story of clairvoyant Lees. See *Daily express.*

Atholl, Justin *Who was Jack the Ripper?* in *Reynolds news* (London) of September 15th 1946. He was an epileptic medical student.

Barnard, Allan (editor) *The harlot killer: the story of Jack the Ripper in fact and fiction* 248 p. Dodd Mead (New York) 1953. Anthology of more or less relevant pieces.

Baverstock, Keith *Footsteps through London's past: a 'discovering' guide* 56p. Shire Pubs. (London) 1972. The Ripper walks are on pages 4-10.

Beattie, John *The Yorkshire Ripper story* 160p. Quartet (London) 1981. This account of the recent spate of murders concludes with two pages on the East End crimes.

Beaumont, F. A. *The fiend of East London: Jack the Ripper* pp. 243-56 of *The fifty most amazing crimes of the last 100 years* 768 p. Odhams (London) 1936. Describes six murders then tails off into the Matters theory.

Bell, Donald *'Jack the Ripper' — the final solution?* in *The Criminologist* vol. 9 no. 33 (Summer 1974) p. 40-61. Conjectures that Dr. Thomas Neill Cream bought himself out of an American prison, performed the Ripper murders (and one on a boy in Portsmouth), then returned to America and took up poisoning.

Bermant, Chaim *Point of arrival: a study of London's East End* 292 p. Eyre Methuen (London) 1975. Chapter nine discusses the suggestion that the killer was a Jew.

Binney, Cecil *Crime and abnormality* 176 p. Oxford U.P. (Oxford) 1949. Relays an account of the Ripper as a religious maniac who conducted open-air services on Margate beach. (Pages 78-9)

Bloch, Ivan *Sexual life in England past and present* 664p. Aldor (London) 1938. "Said to have been identified as an insane student." (p. 445)

Blundell, Nigel *The world's greatest mysteries* 224p. Octopus (London) 1980. A good six page summary of the main theories.

Boar, Roger and Blundell, Nigel *The world's most infamous murders* 192p. Octopus (London) 1983. Pages 92-7 offer the Druitt theory and some *Illustrated police news* pictures.

Borchard, Edwin Montefiore *Convicting the innocent: errors of criminal justice ...* with the collaboration of E. Russell Lutz 421 p. Yale U. Institute of Human Relations (Connecticut) 1932. Chapter on *Frenchy: Ameer Ben Ali* which links the Algerian with the Ripper, reprinted in Barnard.

Brewer, E. Cobham *A dictionary of phrase and fable* 1158 p. Cassell (London) 1970. This edition of the standard work of reference was edited by Sir Ifor Evans and has modified its earlier attribution of nine murders in speaking of "a series of murders ... also rhyming slang for kipper".

Brewer, John Francis, See CONTEMPORARY RECORDS.

Brock, Alan St. H. *A Casebook of crime* 169 p. Rockcliff (London) 1948. Recites the known facts.

Brookes, John Alfred Rowland *Murder in fact and fiction* 284p. Hurst and Blackett (London) 1925. Mentions MacNaghten's suspects and concludes that the murders were "probably the work of a doctor or medical student." (p. 116-7)

Browne, Douglas G. *The rise of Scotland Yard: a history of the Metropolitan Police* 392 p. Harrap (London) 1956. Lists the pertinent facts.

Butler, Arthur *Was Jack the Ripper a woman?* in the *Sun* (London) August 29th-September 1st 1972. A former Chief Superintendent introduces a variation on Stewart's theory involving a female abortionist and male accomplice. Starts strongly but peters out for lack of evidence.

Butler, Ivan *Murderers' London* 238p. Hale (London) 1973. The opening chapter tours 'The Ripper streets'. Factually sound.

Camps, Francis E. *More about Jack the Ripper* in *London Hospital gazette* April 1966, reprinted in the *Criminologist* (London) Februry 1968 and in *Camps on crime* 181p. David and Charles (Newton Abbott) 1973. Includes a plan and pencil sketches of a victim.

Camps, Francis E. and Barber, Richard *The investigation of murder* 143 p. Joseph (London) 1966. The Professor of Forensic Medicine at London University devotes his opening chapter to the Ripper considered from the viewpoint of detection methods used. Concludes that the murderer may not have been caught even using modern methods.

Cargill, David and Holland, Julian *Scenes of murder: a London guide* 230 p. Heinemann (London) 1964. Records the locations of the murders.

Chambers' guide to London the secret city 160p. Ocean Books (London) 1974. The author has four pages on the Ripper, concludes that he was a female abortionist and claims the theory as his own!

Chester, Lewis, Leitch, David and Simpson, Colin *The Cleveland Street affair* 236p. Weidenfeld and Nicolson (London) 1976. Found no evidence for the Duke of Clarence as the Ripper.

Chicago sunday times-herald April 28th 1895. Knight quotes an article entitled *Capture of Jack the Ripper* in which Dr. Howard discloses that the Ripper was another doctor who was declared insane and incarcerated. Includes the earliest known version of the Lees theory. (Transcript provided by J.H.H.Gaute)

Clark-Kennedy, Archibald Edmund *The London: a study of the voluntary hospital system. Volume 2. The second hundred years 1840-1948* 310p. Pitman (London) 1963. Covers the usual ground.

Crowley, Aleister *The confessions of Aleister Crowley: an autohagiography* Abridged edition by John Symonds and Kenneth Grant 1058p. Cape (London) 1969; Hill and Wang (New York) 1970. Originally six volumes of which two were published as *The spirit of solitude* in 1929. Page 755 records the view that the

Ripper committed seven murders to obtain supreme black magic power by forming a Calvary cross of seven points. After the third killing he achieved invisibility!

Cullen, Tom A. *Autumn of terror: Jack the Ripper, his crimes and times* 254 p. Bodley Head (London) 1965. Illustrated. American edition published as *When London walked in terror* Houghton (Boston) 1965. The 1966 British paperback edition was reprinted as *The crimes and times of Jack the Ripper* in 1973. A painstaking book which considers various theories and identifies "for the first time" the three prime suspects. Has Montague Druitt, a barrister, as the killer.

Daily dispatch (Manchester) April 10th 1905, p. 5 *Jack the Ripper: a startling confession in New York*. Charles Y. Hermann takes a bow but "police believe that the man is suffering from hallucinations".

Daily express (London) *How I caught Jack the Ripper!* March 7th 1931 p. 7; *Clairvoyant who tracked Jack the Ripper* March 9th 1931 p. 3; *Jack the Ripper's end* March 10th 1931 p. 3. Three articles tell how Robert James Lees tracks down the killer, a prosperous West End doctor who was certified insane by a "commission de lunatico inquirendo" after his seventeenth murder.

Davis, Derek *'Jack the Ripper' — the handwriting analysis* in the *Criminologist* vol. 9 no. 33 Summer 1974 pp.62-69. Examines two Ripper letters and asserts that both were written by poisoner Dr. Cream "using as much disguise as possible". Or could it have been someone else using not quite as much disguise as possible?

Deacon, Richard *A history of the British secret service* 440 p. Muller (London) 1969. Pages 29-30 recount the Le Queux story. Deacon is a pseudonym of Donald McCormick.

Deacon, Richard *A history of the Russian secret service* 568 p. Muller (London) 1972. Donald McCormick has another go at his theory.

Dearden, Harold *Who was Jack the Ripper?* in *Great unsolved crimes* by A. J. Alan and others. 351 p. Hutchinson (London) 1935. Ephemeral treatment. Attributes the murders to "some doctor or medical student".

Dictionnaire de sexologie: sexologie-lexikon. Sexologie générale, sexualité, contre-sexualité, érotismé, érotologie, bibliographie universelle. 568 p. J. J. Pauvert (Paris) 1962. After such a delightful title it is disappointing to find the article on *Jack l'eventreur* so pedestrian (even *terre à terre*).

Dilnot, George *Scotland Yard: its history and organisation 1829-1929* 351 p. Bles (London) 1929. Brief summary.

Douglas, Arthur *Will the real Jack the Ripper* 72p. Countryside Pubs. (Chorley, Lancs.) 1979. Illustrated. His account of the murders concentrates on the discrepancies in other commentaries. Decides that the Ripper was "a mere nobody after all."

Douthwaite, Louis Charles *Mass murder* 288 p. Long (London) 1928. Disposes of the Deeming/Ripper assertion by claiming that "At the time of the ... murders Deeming was in prison".

Dove, Michael *Is this a skeleton in the doctor's cupboard?* Light relief from the *Sunday express* (London) July 19th 1965. Interview with Dr. Robert Druitt "a descendant of Jack the Ripper" who pointed out that "My form of surgery is much less ambitious".

Downie, Robert Angus *Murder in London: a topographical guide to famous crimes* 175p. Barker (London) 1973. Pages 36-9 give the facts and Druitt theory.

Dutton, Thomas. Wrote three unpublished volumes called *Chronicles of crime* according to McCormick.

Ehrlich, Blake *London on the Thames* 435 p. Cassell (London) 1968. Pages 373-6 have a transient account based on McCormick.

Eisler, Robert *Man into wolf: an anthropological interpretation of sadism, masochism and lycanthropy* ... 286p. Routledge (London) 1951. Makes a passing reference in support of the possibility that the Ripper was a woman.

Empire news (Manchester) October 28th 1923 p. 1-2 *New story of Jack the Ripper.* An "*Empire news* student of criminology" asserted that "Every head of police knows that Jack the Ripper died in Morris Plains lunatic asylum in 1902". The Ripper as Mr. Fogelma a Norwegian sailor.

Encyclopaedia Britannica 1977. Entry on Jack the Ripper in the *Micropaedia*. "At least seven" murders are claimed but no theories are mentioned.

Faith, Nicholas *Jacob the Ripper* in the *Sunday times* (London) February 9th 1975. Report of Bermant's book.

Farson, Daniel *The Hamlyn book of horror* 157p. Hamlyn (London) 1977. Eight pages of illustrated text on the Ripper.

Farson, Daniel *Jack the Ripper* 144p. Joseph (London) 1972. Arrives at the same conclusion as Cullen, but by a somewhat different route. More evidence is offered against M. J. Druitt. The first recent book to include photographs of the corpses of Eddowes and Kelly (two of these appeared in Lacassagne). The paperback edition, Sphere (London) 1973, carries additional information.

Farson, Daniel *The strange obsession* in *Men only* (London) vol. 38 no. 6 June 1973 pp. 10-12, 14, 68. More of the same.

Farson, Daniel *The truth, the whole truth* in the London *Evening news* for September 18th-22nd 1972. Five articles on the murders based on his book. Nothing new until part four in which Montague Druitt is identified.

Fishman, William J. *East End Jewish radicals 1875-1914* 336p. Duckworth (London) 1975. Passing references to the Ripper and to the suggestion that he was a Russian anarchist.

Fishman, William J. *The streets of East London* 139p. Duckworth (London) 1979. Four illustrated pages.

Fletcher, Geoffrey *In the steps of Jack the Ripper* in the *Daily telegraph* (London) October 9th 1974 p. 13.

Fox, Richard Kyle See CONTEMPORARY RECORDS.

Franklin, Charles *The world's worst murderers: exciting and authentic accounts of the great classics of murder* 320p. Odhams (London) 1965. Pages 13-23 sketch in the events and the theories then current. Suggests that the Ripper may have 'retired' after the Kelly killing.

Gardiner, Dorothy *Jack the Ripper* in *Encyclopaedia Americana* (New York) 1977. Sound account says that he was "thought to have murdered 6 or 7". No reference to recent theories.

Gaute, Joseph H. H. and Odell, Robin *Murder 'whatdunit': an illustrated account of the methods of murder* 247p. Harrap (London) 1982. Jack is the only murderer to receive an entry under his own name (p.138-40).

Gaute, Joseph H. H. and Odell, Robin *The murderer's who's who: outstanding international cases from the literature of murder in the last 150 years* 269p. Harrap (London) 1979. Includes two pages on the crimes and favourite suspects and a passing reference to the subject by Colin Wilson in his introduction.

Gillman, Peter *My knife's so nice and sharp* in the *Radio times* (London) July 5th 1973. Surveys the scene for the Jones and Lloyd television series.

Goodman, Jonathon *Bloody versicles: the rhymes of crime* 224 p. David and Charles (Newton Abbot, UK) 1971. Three pages on the Ripper ditties.

Green, Jonathon *The directory of infamy: the best of the worst* 288p. Mills and Boon (London) 1980. A small entry on the master.

Gribble, Leonard Reginald *Jack the Ripper* in *Chambers' encyclopaedia* (London) 1966. Ascribed six deaths to the Ripper.

Gribble, Leonard Reginald *The man they thought was Jack the Ripper* in *True detective* (London) March 1977 pp. 4-12, 49. George Chapman examined and dismissed.

Gribble, Leonard Reginald *Was Jack the Ripper a black magician?* in *True detective* (London) January 1973 pp. 16-25. An illustrated and inaccurate account explores this idea.

Griffiths, Arthur George Frederick *Mysteries of police and crime* volume one 464 p. Cassell (London) 1898. Records three suspects — a Polish Jew, a Russian doctor and a doctor who was later found drowned. Passing references only in one of three pretentious volumes.

Haines, Max *Crime flashback: book 2* 230p. Toronto Sun (Canada) 1981. 8 pages on the Ripper. Supports Druitt.

Harris, Melvin *The murders and the medium* in *The unexplained: mysteries of mind, space and time* 65 (1981) 1290-3. Illustrated article in this part-work looks at and dismisses the Lees legend.

Harrison, Fraser *The dark angel: aspects of Victorian sexuality* 288p. Sheldon Press (London) 1977. Jack rates only two pages but is credited with eight murders.

Harrison, Michael *The world of Sherlock Holmes* 227p. Muller (London) 1973.

Pages 129-138 are the rather unlikely place chosen for repetition of the Stephen theory. See BIOGRAPHIES.

Herd, Richard *The secret of ex-convict SY5 45* in the London *Evening news* September 8th 1955. Old lag's tale of his wife as Jill the Ripper.

Hibbert, Christopher *The roots of evil: a social history of crime and punishment* 524 p. Weidenfeld and Nicolson (London) 1963. Passing account of events.

Hill, William Boyle *A new earth and a new heaven* 312 p. Watts (London) 1936. pp. 119-27 of this spiritualist book recount the Lees story as reported by the *Daily express*.

Honeycombe, Gordon *The murders of the Black Museum 1870-1970* 296p. Hutchinson (London) 1982. Pages 5-14 outline the events and regurgitate some of the usual illustrations. He favours Druitt.

Hubler, Richard Gibson *A stunning explanation of the Jack the Ripper riddle* in *Coronet* (New York) November 1956 pp. 100 -106.

Hynd, Alan Article in *True magazine* (New York) 1956 has Griffith S. Salway discovering a Spanish Ripper's identity via a trunk with a false bottom. Reprinted in the Stuart James novel.

Hynd, Alan *Murder unlimited* in *Good housekeeping* (New York) February 1945 pp. 29, 197-200. Describes contacts between Mathew Parker (a fruiterer) and the Ripper in otherwise orthodox account. Reprinted in Barnard.

Inglis, Norman *Was Jack the Ripper caught?* in *Tit-bits* (London) May 12th 1962. A sighting.

Jack the Ripper: the story of the Whitechapel murders in *Famous crimes past and present* (London) 1903 vol. 2 no. 15 pp. 25-30, no. 16 pp. 49-58, no. 17 pp. 73-81, no. 18 pp. 97-102. Published by Harold Furniss. Jack is "a lunatic suffering from erotomania . . . he was a doctor, not Neill Cream, was mad, and is now probably dead." (Publication made available by J. H. H. Gaute.)

Jannino, E. A. *Jack the Ripper.* Paper presented to a discussion session at the Third International Meeting on Forensic Pathology, London 1963. Postulated 'moon madness' theory for Boston and Whitechapel murders.

Jones, Elwyn and Lloyd, John *The Ripper file* 204p. Futura/Barker (London) 1975. The book of the television series (q.v.). Ignore the Barlow and Watt linking passages and this represents one of the best collections of factual readings on the case, complete with the Freemason conspiracy and Sickert theories. (See Stephen Knight below)

Keating, P. J. *Fact and fiction in the East End* in *The Victorian city: images and realities: vol. 2* edited by H. J. Dyos and Michael Wolff, Routledge (London) 1973. Suggests (pp. 594-5) that the murders reinforced an image of the East End as violent and outcast rather than monotonous and outcast.

Kelly, Alexander Garfield *Ripperature search* in *Assistant librarian* January 1973 pp. 3-6. Describes how the first edition of this bibliography was compiled.

Knight, Stephen *The brotherhood: the secret world of the Freemasons* 336p. Granada (London) 1984. Four page reiteration of bits of his earlier book.

Knight, Stephen *Jack the Ripper: the final solution* in the *Evening news* (London) June 21st (pp. 15-17), 22nd (pp. 12-13), 23rd (pp. 10-11), 24th (12-13), 25th (16-17) 1976. Adapted from the book by Arthur Pottersman and Simon Brodbeck.

Knight, Stephen *Jack the Ripper: the final solution* 284p. Harrap (London) 1976. Illustrated. Painter Walter Sickert, Sir William Gull and John Netley go to endless trouble to eliminate four prostitutes who were party to Royal blackmail. As with many Ripper writers he is stronger when demolishing other people's theories than in presenting his own. An interesting 'solution' although Maurice Richardson found it "so transcendentally preposterous that it deserves a room to itself in the Munchausen Museum of Pseudologia Fantastica." Despite this review a paperback edition was published by Granada in 1977.

Knight, Stephen *Why Sickert denied Ripper tale* in the *Sunday times* (London) July 2nd 1978. His reply to David May (q.v.).

Lacassagne, Jean Alexandre Eugene *Vacher L'Eventreur et les crimes sadiques* 314 p. Storck (Lyons); Masson (Paris) 1899. Pages 254-265 carry MacDonald's account for comparison with the crimes of Joseph Vacher. Notable for photographs of the Kelly and Eddowes corpses.

Le Queux, William *Things I know about kings, celebrities, and crooks* 320 p. Nash and Grayson (London) 1923. Covered the events for *The Globe*. Quotes from "Rasputin's own manuscript" which revealed the Ripper as Dr. Alexander Pedachenko. See also McCormick.

Linklater, Magnus *Did Jack the Ripper have royal blood?* in the *Sunday times* (London) November 1st 1970. Elaborates on the Stowell theory naming Edward, Duke of Clarence as the suspect.

Lithner, Klas *Vem var Jack Uppskäraren?* (Who was Jack the Ripper?) in *Jury* (Stockholm) no. 2 1973 pp. 12-16. Surveys the case and theories.

Logan, Guy B. H. *Masters of crime: studies of multiple murders* 288 p. Paul (London) 1928. Chapter on the Ripper concludes that he was a victim of syphilis from America who had "declared war on the special class from which he chose his victims".

Lustgarten, Edgar *The illustrated story of crime* 223p. Weidenfeld and Nicolson (London) 1976. Pages 208-13 give a brief resumé of the case, with pictures.

McCormick, (George) Donald (King) *The identity of Jack the Ripper* 192 p. Jarrolds (London) 1959; second edition 256 p. Long (London) 1970. Illustrated. Detailed account of the murders and leading suspects. Postulates Dr. Alexander Pedachenko as a Czarist secret agent who committed the murders to discredit London anarchists. Colin Wilson commented that he "accepts the evidence of Le Queux ... a pathological liar", but this claim is refuted in the second edition.

McCormick, (George) Donald (King) *Jack the Ripper* in *Collier's encyclopaedia* 1981. Advances his own theory!

MacDonald, Arthur *Le criminel type dans quelques formes graves de la criminalite* Storck (Lyons) 1893. Includes an account of eleven Ripper murders between 1887 and 1889.

MacDonald, Arthur *Criminology* 416 p. Funk and Wagnalls (New York) 1893. The pioneering American criminologist found that "the atrocities ... are without doubt caused by a pathological sexual passion."

McGowan, Bill *Who was Jack the Ripper?* in the London *Evening news* September 1st 1964 p. 7. Various conjectures including the Ripper as a woman, policeman, mad surgeon, American sailor. Quotes Woodhall's version.

MacLeod, C. M. *A Ripper handwriting analysis* in the *Criminologist* (London) August 1968 pp.120-7. A Canadian graphologist analysed two letters reproduced in the Camps article and concluded that they were written by different people, the first of whom may have been the Ripper "a latent homosexual".

Madison, Arnold *Great unsolved cases* 88p. Franklin Watts (London) 1978. Includes a dull Ripper chapter.

Marx, Roland *L'enigme Jack l'Eventreur* in *L'Histoire* 62 (Dec. 1983) pp. 10-21. Detailed review of the facts, theories and fictional variations.

Masters, R. E. L. and Lea, Eduard *Sex crimes in history: evolving concepts of sadism, lust-murder, and necrophilia from ancient to modern times* 323 p. Julian P. (New York) 1963. Pages 81-8 attribute 9 (and possibly 20) murders which "were not committed without a certain redeeming grace, a saving wit, a mitigating sophistication and savoir faire"(!).

Matters, Leonard W. *The mystery of Jack the Ripper* 254 p. Allen (London) 1929. Illustrated. Variously reprinted since. The first classic work on the subject has a conjectural theory based on a confession relayed at secondhand. The murderer is a doctor revenging his son.

Matters, Leonard W. *Will we ever solve the mystery of Jack the Ripper?* in the *Sunday express* (London) May 4th 1930. Discusses the Chapman/Ripper proposition and refutes it because "it is directly opposed to my own theory".

May, David *Jack the Ripper 'solution' was a hoax, man confesses* in the *Sunday times* (London) June 18th 1978. Joseph Sickert disowns the Stephen Knight story.

Menard, Peter *Certain connections or affinities with Jack the Ripper* 28 p. Nimmo (Edinburgh) 1903. Quotes editorial of Shaw and contemporary criminal statistics to prove that the murders were unconnected crimes used by the government to divert attention from the social conditions of the poor.

Millward, Mervyn *The terror of the East End* in *Police review* (London) August 14th 1936 p.143. Fanciful account of six murders.

Moore, James and Dahl, Norman *Famous lives: crime and justice* 94p. Hamlyn (London) 1980. A short item.

Morland, Nigel *Jack the Ripper: a final word* in the *Criminologist* (London) autumn 1971 pp. 48-9. A handwriting analysis by Prof. C. L. Wilson showed "no justification whatsoever for identifying Jack the Ripper with the Duke of Clarence".

Moylan, John *Scotland Yard and the Metropolitan Police* 398p. Putnam (London) 1929. The former Receiver to the Metropolitan Police said that "It is almost certain that he escaped by committing suicide".

Muusmann, Carl *Hvem var Jack the Ripper?* 102p. Hermann-Petersen (Copenhagen) 1908. He was Alois Szemeredy, a Hungarian who perfected his art in Argentina and eventually in Austria. He committed suicide.

Nash, Jay Robert *Compendium of world crime* 452p. Harrap (London) 1983. Originally published as *Almanac of world crime* 433p. Anchor/Doubleday (New York) 1981. Skimpy treatment of the case (3 pages plus 5 passing references). Favours Cream.

Neil, Charles (editor) *The world's greatest mysteries* 50 p. Neil (Australia) (c. 1936) pp. 5-19 *How Jack the Ripper was caught* retells the clairvoyant Lees story. See the *Daily express.*

Neustatter, Walter Lindesay In the foreword to *Jack the Ripper in fact and fiction* by Robin Odell, Neustatter dismissed various medical theories before suggesting that the Ripper may have been schizophrenic.

New York world telegraph and sun February 15th 1960. The killer as Alonzo Maduro from South America. See McCormick p. 173.

Newton, H. Chance *Crime and the drama or dark deeds dramatized* 284p. S. Paul (London) 1927. Refers to brief performances of "horrible dramatic depictions of certain of the unspeakable murders committed by Jack the Ripper."

Nicholson, Michael *The Yorkshire Ripper* 197p. Star W. H. Allen (London) 1979. Has a four page account of the Whitechapel murders.

Oddie, S. Ingleby *Inquest* 255 p. (London) 1941. pp. 57-62. Describes seven crimes and Oddie's visit to the sites with Conan Doyle. Notes Arthur Diosy's theory that the murders were part of a black magic ritual and the objects found at the scenes of crime formed magical 'pentacles'.

Odell, Robin (Ian) *Jack the Ripper in fact and fiction* 275 p. Harrap (London) 1965. Illustrated. The first thorough book on the subject. Examines the major suggestions, quoting at length from some protagonists. Advances the argument that Jack was a shochet or Jewish slaughterman. A revised paperback edition was published by Mayflower in 1966.

O'Donnell, Bernard. Wrote an unpublished book ascribing the Ripper's activities to a black magician named Roslyn D'Onston according to Whittington-Egan (q.v.)

O'Donnell, Elliott *Great Thames mysteries* 288 p. Selwyn and Blount (London) 1929. A chapter on the Ripper speculating about links between the murders and cases of dismemberment in 1887-8.

O'Donnell, Elliott *Haunted Britain* 192 p. Rider (London) 1948. p. 36 has accounts of ghostly events in Whitechapel, recorded in 1895.

Olsson, Jan Olof *Generaler och likstallda* (Stockholm) 1970. Pages 16-23 recount Cullen's theory as told to the author.

O'Neil, P. *Parting shots: Clarence the Ripper?* in *Life* (New York) November 13th 1970 pp. 85-8. Speculation on the Duke of Clarence theory. See Stowell, Thomas.

Paley, Bruce *A new theory on the Jack the Ripper murders* in *True crime monthly* April 1982 pp. 3-13. Now it is the turn of Joseph Barnett, who is at least known to have met (and lived with) Mary Kelly.

Parrish, J. M. and Crossland, John R. (editors). See F. A. Beaumont.

Pearsall, Ronald *The worm in the bud: the world of Victorian sexuality* 560 p. Weidenfeld and Nicolson (London) 1969. Pages 306-13 provide an account of the murders with a wealth of background material some of it rather remote e.g. "During the crucial year twenty-seven policemen had died, mainly of exposure to the elements, and 131 had been taken off their beats with sore feet". Claims 9 murders.

Pearson. Edmund Lester *More studies in murder* 232 p. Random House (New York) 1936. A chapter on the murders is reprinted in Barnard. Adds nothing except a delightful comment on the theory of Matters. "The deathbed confession bears about the same relation to the facts of criminology as the exploits of Peter Rabbit ... to zoology".

The People (London) May 19th 1895 *A startling story*. Relays the Lees theory from the *Chicago sunday times - herald*, according to Whittington-Egan.

People's journal September 26th 1919. Rumbelow (q.v.) quotes an item about the retirement of a detective named Steve White who had seen and almost arrested the Ripper.

Pimlott, John Alfred Ralph *Toynbee Hall: fifty years of social progress 1884-1934* 315p. Dent (London) 1935. Pages 81-2 describe the efforts of a vigilance association to apprehend the Ripper.

Platnick, Kenneth B. *Great mysteries of history* 224p. David and Charles (Newton Abbot) 1972. The main themes appear on pages 58-73.

Prothero, Margaret *The history of the Criminal Investigation Department at Scotland Yard from earliest times until today* 319 p. Jenkins (London) 1931. Only two pages on the murders, one quoting a letter by Queen Victoria. See BIOGRAPHIES.

The Reader's digest book of strange stories, amazing facts 608p. Reader's Digest (London) 1975. Three pages on the crimes.

Reilly, B. E. *Jack the Ripper: the mystery solved?* in *City* (City of London Police magazine) February 1972. 'Doctor Merchant' is condemned because of his home (Brixton) and date of death (1888) although no evidence is offered that he had ever been to Whitechapel! Illustrated by pictures of a knife "claimed to have belonged to Jack the Ripper".

Revill, Joan *Read all abaht it. The 'orrible 'oroscope of Jack the Ripper* in *Prediction* (London) June 1973 pp. 6-9. Yes, it could have been M. J. Druitt — or the Crown Prince of Austria!

Reynolds news and sunday citizen (London) February 8th 1959 p. 9 *Blacksmith gives Yard vital clue: Jack the Ripper was my cousin.* The Ripper as Frank Edwards, cousin of a retired Worthing blacksmith.

Richardson, Joseph Hall *From the City to Fleet Street: some journalistic experiences* 302 p. S. Paul (London) 1927. Describes the case, quotes a letter from Anderson and a description of the Ripper in the *Police gazette* (London). Cites the *Star* of 1924 (?) in refutation of Le Queux.

Robertson, Terence *Madman who murdered nine women* in *Reynolds news and sunday citizen* October 29th 1950 p. 3. Journalistic rehash of the nine murders committed by a Polish sailor.

Robinson, Tom *The Whitechapel horrors: being an authentic account of the Jack the Ripper murders* 32p. Daisy Bank Pub. (Manchester) (no date). Attributes seven murders to the killer. (Information supplied by Michel Parry)

Rosenwater, Irving *Jack the Ripper - sort of a cricket person?* in the *Cricketer* January 1973 pp. 6-7, 22. Information about M. J. Druitt's cricketing career. The title refers to that of E. W. Swanton's autobiography. (Mr Rosenwater informed me that he was unable to discover whether Druitt was left-handed. See Farson)

Rowe, Peter *see* Vincent, William

Rumbelow, Donald *The City of London Police museum and exhibition* in *Police journal* (Chichester) July 1970 pp. 343-4. Reports that Metropolitan Police were forbidden to disturb Kelly corpse before the arrival of bloodhounds, Meanwhile City Police entered the premises and took photographs. Four photographs of the body of Eddowes are in the museum.

Rumbelow, Donald *The complete Jack the Ripper* 286p. W. H. Allen (London) 1975. Illustrated. The best book yet. Offers no new theory but Colin Wilson's introduction adds artist Frank Miles to the roll of dishonour. The paperback edition (Star: 1976) lacks both introduction and index.

Sabben-Clare, James *Jack the Ripper* in the *Trusty servant* no. 34 December 1972 pp. 3-5. The Old Wykehamist magazine celebrates one of its distinguished old boys — M. J. Druitt.

Saxon, Peter *The man who dreamed of murder* in *Sexton Blake library* November 3rd 1958. Medium Lees rides again.

Scott, Harold (editor) *The concise encyclopaedia of crime and criminals* Deutsch (London) 1961. Ripper article appears to have been written by McCormick.

Shew, Edward Spencer *A companion to murder* 303 p. Cassell (London) 1960; Knopf (New York) 1962. Repeats the evidence of Adam that Chapman may have been the Ripper.

Sims, George Robert *The mysteries of modern London* 192 p. Pearson (London)

1906. Passing references to the Ripper "a man of birth and education".

Sitwell, Osbert *Noble essences of courteous revelations: being a book of characters and the fifth and last volume of left hand, right hand* MacMillan (London) 1950. Pages 189-91 record painter Walter Sickert's claim to have lived in lodgings formerly occupied by the killer, a veterinary student who died in Bournemouth.

Sparrow, Gerald *Crimes of passion* 154p. Barker (London) 1973. Pages 90-8 carry a thoroughly slipshod rehash of the Clarence theory with at least fifteen mistakes in four pages.

Spiering, Frank *Prince Jack: the true story of Jack the Ripper* 192p. Doubleday (New York) 1978. A careless elaboration of Stowell's theory. Jack was the Duke of Clarence but J. K. Stephen wrote the letters. No sources are quoted for many significant statements but other books (including this bibliography) are freely pillaged without acknowledgement. Illustrated.

Springfield, Lincoln *Some piquant people* 287p. Fisher Unwin (London) 1924. Claimed that the finger was levelled at 'Leather Apron' by Harry Dam, a journalist on the *Star* and that when Pizer was released from custody they headed off any libel suit by paying him £10 "being little more than a pound a murder."

Stewart, William *Jack the Ripper: a new theory* 223 p. Quality Press (London); Saunders (Toronto) 1939. Argued that the Ripper was a woman. The second major book on the theme.

Stewart-Gordon, James *The enduring mystery of Jack the Ripper* in *Reader's digest* July 1973 pp. 87-91. The mixture as before.

Stowell, Thomas E. A. *Jack the Ripper – a solution?* in the *Criminologist* (London) November 1970. Announced that the murders were committed by 'S' "the heir to power and wealth". Subsequent reports suggested that S was the Duke of Clarence but Stowell denied this. Also discusses the clairvoyant Lees story and recounts details about Sir William Gull the royal physician.

Stowell, Thomas E. A. In a letter to the *Times* published on November 5th 1970, denied that Clarence was his suspect but repeated that "he was a scion of a noble family". Stowell died on the previous day and his son destroyed the Ripper papers (according to the *Times* of November 14th).

Sunday chronicle (Manchester) of February 6th 1949 *She was a decoy to catch Jack the Ripper*. Concerns Mrs. Amelia Brown, a police whistle, and a rope dropped over the wall of the London Hospital.

Symonds, John *The great beast: the life and magick of Aleister Crowley* 413 p. MacDonald (London) 1971. First published in 1951 this edition contains chapters from *The magic of Aleister Crowley* (1958). A previously unpublished note on p. 16 says "The Victorian worthy in the case of Jack the Ripper was no less a person than Helena Petrovna Blavatsky". Not unnaturally Symonds describes the notion as preposterous.

Symons, Julian Gustave *Crime and detection: an illustrated history from 1840* 288p. Studio Vista (London) 1966. Two pages with illustrations. American edition entitled *A pictorial history of crime* Crown (New York) 1966.

Symons, Julian Gustave *The criminal classes*. A chapter in *Rule Britannia: the Victorian world* 255p. Times Newspapers (London) 1974 edited by George Perry and Nicholas Mason. Two pages on the Ripper including several pictures. Claims six murders.

Thomson, Basil *The Story of Scotland Yard* 324 p. Grayson (London) 1935. Page 178 mentions the case and reports that CID officers suspected an insane Russian doctor who committed suicide in 1888.

Thorwald, Jurgen *The marks of Cain* 239 p. Thames and Hudson (London) 1965. Pages 65-6 record the principal facts and the McCormick theory.

Time (New York) *Who was Jack the Ripper?* November 9th 1970 p. 29. Speculation on the Clarence supposition. See Stowell, Thomas.

The Times of November 4th 1970 p. 12 *Court circular clears Clarence*. "A loyalist on the staff at Buckingham Palace" cites court circulars which suggest that (Albert Victor) Edward was otherwise engaged at the times of the murders.

The Times of August 16th 1973. *New Ripper* previews an episode of the B.B.C. Television series in which Joseph Sickert accuses Sir William Gull of political murders.

Two worlds (London) February 21st 1959 *Medium solved Britain's vilest murders*. The Lees story. See *Daily express*.

Umpire (Manchester) July 31st 1910 p. 2 *Who was Jack the Ripper?* Dr. Forbes Winslow appeared before Bow Street magistrate Mr. Marsham on behalf of William Grant, an Irish medical student turned cattle-boat fireman, who had served a prison sentence for wounding a Whitechapel woman. The article implied that London solicitor George Kebbell had appeared for Grant at his preliminary hearing and had later announced not only that Grant was the Ripper but that he died in prison! Winslow reported receipt of a 'confession' from the Melbourne former fiancée of the Ripper who had also denounced her beloved to the Australian ,police with the result that 'Jack' emigrated to South Africa. Interviewed after the hearing Winslow gave his suspect as "an epileptic maniac" who "wore Canadian snowshoes" for quietness.

Vincent, William *Jack the Ripper* in the *Police review* (London) December 16th 1977-April 14th 1978.

> 16th December 1977 pp. 1748-9 *New series starting this week. Slums of shame*
>
> 23rd December 1977 pp. 1780-1 *Death of an unfortunate. Was Emma the first victim?*
>
> 6th January 1978 pp.16-17 *Slaying of a soldiers 'sweetheart'. Martha's murder more than a coincidence*
>
> 13th January 1978 pp. 54-5 *Drunkard joins the death trail … and a talented detective joins the hunt*
>
> 20th January 1978 pp. 90-1 *Slit throat and abdomen set pattern. Witch – hunt is on for Leather Apron Jack*

27th January 1978 pp. 130-1 *Dark Annie – death in a pool of blood. Plot thickens amid power struggle*

3rd February 1978 pp. 166-7 *Strong rap from the Coroner. Suspects arrested and set free*

10th February 1978 pp. 202-3 *Confessions of a cool killer? Or letters from expert hoaxers?*

24th February 1978 pp. 274-5 *Dutfield's Yard mystery. The missing hours to murder*

3rd March 1978 pp. 310-1 *Second murder of a night, the drunk who met death*

10th March 1978 pp. 350-1 *Letters from the Ripper and ... the writing on the wall*

17th March 1978 pp. 380-1 *The 'bloodiest' killing and then ... an illegal cover – up or lawful witholding of facts*

24th March 1978 pp. 442-3 *Narrow escape and two more killings. Suicide, suspicion and a confession*

31st March 1978 pp. 478-9 *An anniversary killing? The torso without a name*

4th April 1978 pp. 520-1 *The last killing and ... the arrest of a blood-stained seaman*

14th April 1978 pp.554-5 *Suspects line up, now . . . can you pick out the Ripper?*

A detailed review of the main facts and theories. Concludes that they amount to very little.

Volta, Ornella *The vampire:* translated from the Italian by Raymond Rudorff 160p. Tandem (London) 1965. Claims 9 murders for the Ripper between 1887-9, most of her other facts are equally shaky. He "showed a surrealist sense of composition" in arranging intestines!

Von Hentig, Hans *The criminal and his victim* Yale U.P. (New Haven, Conn.) 1948.

Walbrook, H. M. *Murders and murder trials 1812-1912* 366 p. Constable (London) 1932. Surveys the known facts.

Weiskopf, J. S. *Jack the Ripper* in *History makers* (London) January 16th 1970 pp. 432-5. Summary of the case, no theories but two contemporary posters.

Whitmore, Richard *Victorian and Edwardian crime and punishment from old photographs* Batsford (London) 1978. Includes the usual picture of Kelly's corpse.

Whittington-Egan, Richard *A casebook on Jack the Ripper* 174p. Wildy (London) 1976. Reprints the *Contemporary review* articles and extends the coverage through to 1975. An interesting review of the literature. Contains a substantial bibliography lifted largely from the first edition of this one (e.g. the entry for R. W. Hackwood was included here purely because of the 'Digression on eyeballs'. Why was it included there — when the item was published over thirty years before the murders?)

Whittington-Egan, Richard *The identity of Jack the Ripper* in *Contemporary review* (London) November 1972 pp. 239-43; December 1972 pp. 317-21; January 1973 pp. 13-18, 24. Surveys the main theories.

Who was Jack the Ripper? in *Crimes and punishment* (London) no. 17 July 1975 pp. 455-70. Discusses the facts and major theories. Well illustrated. Authoritative as befits a magazine which employed Joe Gaute, Robin Odell, Donald Rumbelow and Colin Wilson.

Williams, Guy R. *The hidden world of Scotland Yard* 270 p. Hutchinson (London) 1972. Pages 28-33 have a brief note on Commissioner Warren's fate and several pictures from contemporary journals.

Wilson, Colin *A casebook of murder* 288p. Frewin (London) 1969; Cowles (New York) 1970. Good arguments against existing propositions. Ascribes a suicidal tendency to the killer indicated by destruction of the womb. Disposes of Odell and Stewart arguments by suggesting that "The essence of the sadistic crime is the fantasy beforehand, and fantasy flourishes in a vacuum". The most imaginative approach so far.

Wilson, Colin *A criminal history of mankind* 702p. Granada (London) 1984. Several references to the Ripper; claims that the Victorians were only dimly aware that these were sex crimes.

Wilson, Colin *The Duke and the Ripper* in *Books and bookmen* (London) December 1972 pp. 92-3. A commentary on the Stephen and Druitt theories based on Harrison and Farson.

Wilson, Colin *My search for Jack the Ripper* series in *Evening standard* (London) in 1960.
August 8th, p. 7 *In a vanishing London I pick up the grim trail of murder.*
August 9th, p. 12 *Amazing – how luck never deserted the killer.*
August 10th, p. 12 *Always, a woman ready to die.*
August 11th, p. 12 *The most sensational crime night of them all.*
August 12th, p. 12 *Now the final question: who was the Ripper?*
Gives the Matters, Adam and McCormick theories.

Wilson, Colin *The occult* 601 p. Hodder (London) 1971. Footnote to p. 446 accuses Volta (q.v.) of wild inaccuracies.

Wilson, Colin *Order of assassins: the psychology of murder* 242 p. Hart Davis (London) 1972. Reprints *Leicester chronicle* article and comments on the Reilly theory.

Wilson, Colin *Rasputin and the fall of the Romanovs* 240 p. Barker (London) Farrar Straus (New York) 1964. Le Queux (q.v.) claimed to have read a manuscript dictated in French by Rasputin and recovered from his cellar, giving the facts behind the Ripper murders. According to Wilson, Rasputin had neither cellar nor French. See pp. 204-6.

Wilson, Colin *Was the Ripper the highest in the land?* in *Leicester chronicle* of

January 28th 1971 pp.14-15. Elaborates on Stowell's theory and confirms that the Duke of Clarence was suspect. Prefers Cullen's view.

Wilson, Colin and Pitman, Patricia *Encyclopaedia of murder* 576 p. Barker (London) 1961. Summary of the main suggestions then on offer about the Ripper's identity.

Woodhall, Edwin Thomas *Crime and the supernatural* 282p. Long (London) 1935. Chapter four has yet another version of the Lees theory.

Woodhall, Edwin Thomas *Jack the Ripper: or when London walked in terror* 96 p. Mellifont Press (London) 1937. Pulp paperback which presents Jill the Ripper as Olga Tchkersoff revenging the death of her prostitute sister, adds another rehash of the Lees story, then lifts Matters's theory. Reaches new heights in a tour de force account of the escape and suicide of a suspect based on a misunderstanding of five lines of MacNaghten. See WHY THE RIPPER?

Wulffen, Erich *Der Sexualverbrecher: ein Handbuch für Juristen, Verwaltungsbeamte und Ärzte* (Berlin) 1922. Eleven murders committed between 1887-9 as a surrogate for the sexual act.

Yallop, David A. *Deliver us from evil* 375p. MacDonald Futura (London) 1981. This book on the Yorkshire Ripper includes five pages outlining Jack's career.

3 BIOGRAPHIES

The autobiographies of people involved in the investigations are generally unhelpful as sources of information about the murderer, exhibiting combinations of hazy recollection, hearsay and ignorance sheltered behind official masks. Some of the memoirs provide interesting 'local colour', including those of Dew, Sir Henry Smith and Halsted.

Anderson, Robert *The lighter side of my official life* 295 p. Hodder (London) 1910. The Head of CID from 1888-1902 lets it be known that Jack was a "low class Polish Jew" and that the letters were "the creation of an enterprising London journalist" but proffers no evidence. Richardson records a letter by Anderson to "one of the daily papers" about the removal of the writing from the wall. See FACTS AND THEORIES.

Anderson, Robert *The lighter side of my official life: XI. At Scotland Yard* in *Blackwood's magazine* (Edinburgh) March 1910. Pages 357-8 give an account similar to that published in book form but a footnote adds that a witness identified the Ripper who was "Caged in an asylum ... but when he learned that the suspect was a fellow-Jew he declined to swear to him".

Barnett, Henrietta Octavia Weston *Canon Barnett: his life, work and friends by his wife* 2 vols. Murray (London) 1918. Second volume has a chapter on Whitechapel conditions when he went there as vicar, including reactions to the Ripper outrages.

Bell, Quentin *Virginia Woolf: a biography. Volume one. Virginia Stephen 1882 – 1912* 230p. Hogarth P. (London) 1972. Details of the madness of cousin James

Kenneth Stephen (p. 35-6).

Buckle, George Earle (editor) *The letters of Queen Victoria: third series. A selection from Her Majesty's correspondence and journal between the years 1886 and 1901. Volume one 1886-1890* 688 p. Murray (London) 1930. Page 447 has the text of a cypher telegram to Lord Salisbury instructing that "these courts must be lit, and our detectives improved". Page 449 carries a draft letter (by Sir Henry Ponsonby) listing "some of the questions that occur to the Queen".

Cathcart, Helen *Lord Snowdon* 208 p. W. H. Allen (London) 1968. Sycophantic biography explains how Dr. Robert Jones (the photographer's grandfather) was launched on his distinguished career by developing "an all absorbing interest in insanity" following the murders. He became the first Medical Superintendent of Claybury hospital in that year.

Cobb, Geoffrey Belton *Critical years at the Yard: the career of Frederick Williamson of the Detective Department and the CID* 251 p. Faber (London) 1956. Recounts top level police reaction to the murders. Critical of Anderson; Williamson took no part.

Dew, Walter *I caught Crippen* 242 p. Blackie (London) 1938. Devotes a third of the book to the Ripper; describes events with plenty of local colour because he was stationed with the CID in Whitechapel. No theory.

Dictionary of national biography Smith, Elder (London) 1898. Entries for J. F. Stephen and his son. See Michael Harrison.

East, John M. *'neath the mask: the story of the East family* 356 p. Allen and Unwin (London) 1967. Refers to an encounter between a stall attendant and a suspect.

Evening news (London) March 5th 1954 p. 6. Obituary of Chief Inspector James Stockley notes that he was disguised as a "loafer, costermonger, milkman, chimney sweep and itinerant musician" as part of Ripper operation.

Ford, Ford Madox *Return to yesterday* 438p. Gollancz (London) 1931. Claims that his nurse, Mrs Atterbury, discovered the body of one of the victims and saw a man vanish into the fog. (What fog?)

George, Earl Lloyd *Lloyd George* 248 p. Muller (London) 1960. Similar account to that by Owen (below).

Halsted, Dennis Gratwick *Doctor in the nineties* 206 p. Johnson (London) 1959. Halsted was at the London Hospital at the time and described the atmosphere and general suspicion which fell on medical men. Outlines six murders and suggests that Jack was a syphilitic sailor of the North Sea fishing fleet. "The great surgical skill which he used ... could easily have been picked up by a man accustomed to boning and filleting fish".

Harrison, Michael *Clarence: the life of the Duke of Clarence and Avondale, KG 1864-1892* 253 p. W. H. Allen (London) 1972. Reattributes Stowell's Clarence theory to J. K. Stephen.

Hyde, H. Montgomery *Carson: the life of Sir Edward Carson, Lord Carson of Duncairn* 515 p. Heinemann (London) 1953. Pages 182-3 link George Chapman with the Ripper citing Chief Inspector Abberline in support.

Jackson, Robert *Francis Camps: famous case histories of the celebrated pathologist* 208p. Hart Davis (London) 1975. Chapter nine *Camps on the Ripper* outlines the events of the time and claims that Camps "came down in favour of the Farson theory."

Kingston, Charles *The bench and the dock* 290p. Stanley Paul (London) 1925. Pages 203-4 describe James Monro's supposed involvement in the Ripper search. Reports the suspects as a West End doctor and a medical student at St. Bartholomew's hospital.

Lamb, David C. *On active service for humanity: he found his soul on Devil's Island* in *Tit-bits* (London) September 23rd 1939 pp. 6-7. The memoirs of the Salvation Army Commissioner recall a sign-writer visitor who had predicted the death of Carroty Nell. Lamb adds "Remembering my visitor's exceptional dexterity, his story of seeing visions of blood, his strange demeanour and his remarkable forecast, I have now little doubt in my mind that he was Jack the Ripper". This is the article referred to by Wilson and Pitman.

Leeson, Benjamin *Lost London: the memoirs of an East End detective* 187 p. S. Paul (London) 1934. Tells how he was called to the scene of the Coles murder, the rest is hearsay. Claims thirteen victims and hints at "a certain doctor, known to me". Includes photograph of Swallow Alley, which cannot compete with those of himself in 'disguise'.

Lowndes, Susan (editor) *Diaries and letters of Marie Belloc Lowndes 1911-1947* 291 p. Chatto and Windus (London) 1971. Pages 96-8 describe origins of *The Lodger* and record Hemingway's enthusiasm for the book.

MacNaghten, Melville L. *Days of my years* 300p. Arnold (London) 1915. Treacly memoirs by a Chief of CID suggest that the "Boss" letter came from a journalist and that the Ripper committed suicide.

Marjoribanks, Edward *The life of Lord Carson. Volume one* 455 p. Gollancz (London) 1932. The life of the great advocate who prosecuted George Chapman the poisoner. Conjectures that Chapman was the Ripper (pp. 304-5).

Marjoribanks, Edward *The life of Sir Edward Marshall Hall* 483 p. Gollancz (London) 1929. Contains anecdotes about Neil Cream who confessed to being the Ripper. Hall dismissed the idea (pp. 48-50).

May, Betty *Tiger-woman: my story* 232p. Duckworth (London) 1929. Written by Bernard O'Donnell, originally as a series of articles for the *World's pictorial news*. Includes an incident in which Aleister Crowley claimed to have the ties of the Ripper, who was a surgeon-magician.

Moore-Anderson, Arthur P. *Sir Robert Anderson and Lady Agnes Anderson* 173p. Marshall, Morgan and Scott (London) 1947. Records the notions that Jack was a Malay seaman on shore leave, that a vital clay pipe was destroyed and that "the only person who ever had a good view of the murderer identified the suspect without hesitation :... but refused to give evidence".

Neil, Arthur Fowler *Forty years of man-hunting* 288 p. Jarrolds (London) 1932. Police Superintendent presents the "strong theory" that poisoner George Chapman was the Ripper.

O'Donnell, Elliott *Confessions of a ghost hunter* 323p. Thornton Butterworth (London) 1928. Tales of Whitechapel hauntings by Lizzie Stride and Mary Kelly (p. 210-11).

Okey, Thomas *A basketful of memoirs: an autobiographal sketch* 152 p. Dent (London) 1930. Reference to two Neapolitan lawyers who wished to see the scene of a Giacomo-la-Squarciatore murder.

Owen, Frank *Tempestuous journey: Lloyd George, his life and times* 784 p. Hutchinson (London) 1954. Tells of Lloyd George's shock at seeing East End conditions on a jaunt to catch the killer.

Sitwell, Osbert (editor) *A free house: or the artist as craftsman, being the writings of Walter Richard Sickert* 362 p. Macmillan (London) 1947. Preface has the same story as recorded in *Noble essences.*

Smith, Henry *From constable to commissioner: the story of sixty years, most of them misspent* 137 p. Chatto and Windus (London) 1910. Smith was Chief Superintendent of Police in the City of London 1885-90 and includes details of the Ripper's City murder and of a rendezvous with a suspect.

Spicer, Robert Clifford *I caught Jack the Ripper* in *Daily express* (London) March 16th 1931. He arrested a doctor who was released by Spicer's police superiors.

Stephen, Leslie *The life of Sir James Fitzjames Stephen, a judge of the High Court of Justice, by his brother* ... 504 p. Smith, Elder (London) 1895. Includes a chapter on James Stephen. See Michael Harrison.

Wensley, Frederick Porter *Forty years of Scotland Yard: the record of a lifetime's service in the Criminal Investigation Department* 312 p. Garden City Pub. Co. (New York) 1930; published in England as *Detective days* Cassell (London) 1931. Describes the near capture of the murderer of Frances Coles and speculates that this may have been the Ripper.

Williams, Montagu *Round London: down East and up West* 387p. MacMillan (London) 1892. Describes his visits to a penny peep-show in the Whitechapel Road showing wax models of the Ripper victims.

Williams, Watkin Wynn *The life of General Sir Charles Warren: by his grandson* 450 p. Blackwell (Oxford) 1941. Pages 221-2 have an unreliable account of murders. Denies that all the victims were prostitutes; describes the Ripper as reticent; claims that Scotland Yard received 1,200 letters daily. Warren's bloodhound tests seen as "very successful" but claims that no murders took place when the bloodhounds were in London. Favours the doctor theory of Griffiths.

Winslow, Lyttleton Stewart Forbes *Recollections of forty-years: being an account at first hand of some famous criminal lunacy cases* ... Ousley (London) 1910. Chapter on the Ripper. Author offered many suggestions to the police including replacement of Whitechapel police by attendants experienced with lunatics. Records the story that Jack was a gorilla. Winslow received several Ripper letters and decided that he was a well-to-do man living near St. Paul's and suffering from religious mania. Claimed to have stopped the murders by publishing his clues.

4 FICTION AND DRAMA

The Whitechapel murders have fascinated authors for years and the distinction between fact and fiction has grown increasingly blurred. Most crime writers seem to have tried their hand at the theme and many attempts were published in ephemeral magazines so no claim can be made that this section is complete. Readers are invited to send in any omissions in case a third edition sees the light. Several classics of Ripperature have established themselves, notably *The Lodger* by Marie Belloc Lowndes and *Ritual in the dark* by Colin Wilson. Two short stories which must be mentioned are Thomas Burke's *The hands of Mr. Ottermole* and *Yours truly, Jack the Ripper* by Robert Bloch, although I prefer his more recent and futuristic *A toy for Juliette*. Sherlock Holmes has shown particular resilience in pursuit of this appropriate adversary, almost succumbing to him in Baring-Gould's 'biography' and Boucher's translation, playing a more familiar role in Ellery Queen's story and even identified with him in several recent stories (but watch out for Dr Watson says John Sladek)! Professor Moriarty takes a hand in Gardner's book but not before a new generation of Rippers is sired by Philip José Farmer. My accolade for variants on the Ripper theme goes to none of these but to a delightful essay in sick humour called *Dulcie* by Hugh Reid.

Alexander, David *Terror on Broadway* 243 p. Random (New York) 1954; Boardman (London) 1956. Jack (call me Waldo) on Times Square.

Alexander, Karl *Time after time* 320p. Granada (London) 1980. The book of the film in which Dr Leslie John Stephenson (alias Jack) is sent into eternity by H. G. Wells. An imaginative idea (involving time travel) but it doesn't come to fruition.

Allen, F. *Whitechapel murder* Ogilvie (USA) (c. 1927). A scarce item of fiction recorded in the *Cumulative book index* for 1928.

Anri, Pol *Jack the Ripper: of eene misgreep. Blijspel in een bedrijf* 44p. Janssens (Antwerp) 1910. One-act comedy in the *Flemish play collections for men* series. Number 242 if you are interested.

Arlen, Michael *Hell! said the duchess: a bed-time story* 181 p. Heinemann (London) 1934. The Jane the Ripper murders.

Avellone, Michael *A theory Holmes would have liked* in the *Daily express* August 2nd 1973. The American thriller writer suggests that Sir Arthur Conan Doyle was the Ripper.

Bailey, L. W. *The case of the unmentioned case: a Sherlock Holmes speculation* in *Listener* (London) December 16th 1965 pp. 98-9. (See also MUSIC AND FILMS) Proves that Sherlock Holmes was the miscreant.

Baring-Gould, William S. *Sherlock Holmes: a biography of the world's first consulting detective* 284 p. Hart-Davis (London) 1962. Chapter XV tells how Holmes (in drag) is almost killed by the Ripper but is rescued by Watson in the nick of time. Revealed as Inspector Athelney Jones.

Barnard, Allan (editor) See FACTS AND THEORIES.

Barnes, Peter *The ruling class: a baroque comedy* 115 p. Heinemann (London) 1969. This tasty play, first performed in 1968, has Jack as "a paranoid-schizophrenic Gurney", the nearest approach to Beelzebub that contemporary drama permits. Is sadism the ultimate sin?

Barry, John Brooks *The Michaelmas girls* 262p. Deutsch (London) 1975. The Ripper teams up with a procuress.

Beeding, Francis *Death walks in Eastrepps* 318 p. Hodder and Stoughton (London) 1931. Six 'orrible murders by the 'Eastrepps Evil'.

Benson, Theodora *In the fourth ward*. Short story about the Ripper in America written in 1930 and included in her *Man from the tunnel and other stories* 271 p. Appleton (New York) 1950. Reprinted in Barnard.

Bloch, Robert *A toy for Juliette* in Harlan Ellison's *Dangerous visions*. Jack as an involuntary time-traveller provides a solution to the *Marie Céleste* mystery in passing.

Bloch, Robert *Yours truly, Jack the Ripper* in his *The opener of the way* Arkham House (Sauk City, USA) 1945. An ageless Ripper stalks his 88th victim in contemporary Chicago. Originally published in *Weird tales* (1943) "It has since pursued me in reprint, collection, anthologies, foreign translations, radio broadcasts and television".

Boucher, Anthony *A kind of madness* in *Ellery Queen's mystery magazine* August 1972 pp. 36–42. The Ripper hung.

Boucher, Anthony *Jack El Distripador* in *Ellery Queen's mystery magazine* (New York) 1945, reprinted in Allan Barnard's *The harlot killer*. Synopsis of Boucher's translation from the Spanish "one of many which originated in Germany and found their way to Spain and Latin America in this fantastically distorted form" (Barnard). Sherlock Holmes is almost the fortieth victim!

Brautigan, Richard *Trout fishing in America: a novel* 151p. Cape (London) 1970. An original explanation as to why the Ripper was never caught — it's all a matter of disguise.

Brecht, Bertolt and Wëill, Kurt (Music) *Die Dreigroschenoper* 1929; translated as *The threepenny opera* 1955. "Owes as much for its inspiration to Jack the Ripper as it does to Gay's *Beggar's opera*." (Cullen).

Brooke, Hugh *Man made angry* 289 p. Longmans (London and New York) 1932. "Founded on the Whitechapel murders . . . according to Basil Hogarth". (Sandoe).

Brown, Fredric *The screaming Mimi* 222 p. Dutton (USA) 1949; Boardman (London) 1950. Chicago setting.

Burke, Thomas *The hands of Mr. Ottermole* in his *The pleasantries of old Quong* 279 p. Constable (London) 1931; published in USA as *A teashop in Limehouse* Little, Brown (Boston) 1931. Reprinted in Barnard. "Mr. Ottermole is a strangler rather than a slasher but his derivation seems clear." (Sandoe).

Burroughs, William S. *Nova express* 251p. Grove (New York) 1962. Jack's murder notes are 'cut' into the text (p.45).

Campbell, Ramsey *Jack's little friend* in Parry, Michel *Jack the knife* p. 130-9.

Capon, Paul *The seventh passenger* 192 p. Ward Lock (London) 1953. The story of the Rosebud killer is loosely modelled on the Ripper theme set in 1952.

Cashman, John *The gentleman from Chicago: being an account of the doings of Thomas Neill Cream* ... 310p. Hamish Hamilton (London) 1974. A first-person account of his career. An appendix dismisses the Cream as Ripper theory because he was in prison at the time.

Cendrars, Blaise *Moravagine* 1926, translation published by Peter Owen (London) 1968. A chapter entitled 'Jack the Ripper' has Moravagine extending his musical scope as the Ripper in Berlin.

Chaplin, Patrice *By Flower and Dean Street and the love apple* Duckworth (London) 1976. Jack returns as an advertising jingle writer.

Chetwynd-Hayes, R. *The gatecrasher* in his *The unbidden* 224 p. Tandem (London) 1971. An uninvited guest at a seance.

Christensen, Flemming *Who's afraid of Big Bad Jack? Or an attempt to disclose the identity of Jack the Ripper* in the *Baker Street journal* (new series) vol. 15 no. 4 December 1965 pp. 229-235.

Who wasn't Turner? in the *Baker Street journal* (new series) vol. 18 no. 2 June 1968 p. 110. Watson did it/them.

Creepy (1968) An American horror comic 'solves' the crimes.

de Lorde, Andre *Jack l'eventreur*. An apparently unpublished play.

de Waal, Ronald Burt *The world bibliography of Sherlock Holmes and Doctor Watson: a classified and annotated list of material relating to their lives and adventures* 526p. Bramhall House (New York) 1974. Includes two pages of Ripper variants on Holmes, Watson or Moriarty as villain/hero. I have 'borrowed' nine of these for inclusion here.

Desmond, Hugh *Death let loose* 189 p. Wright and Brown (London) 1956. The Ripper story retold with the Chief of Police in a leading role.

Desmond, Hugh *A scream in the night* 188 p. Wright and Brown (London) 1955. A modern Ripper preying on children.

Desnos, Robert *La liberté ou l'amour! suivi de deuil pour deuil* 160 p. Gallimard (France) 1927. Features the Ripper.

Dettman, Bruce *Who wasn't Jack the Ripper?* in the *Baker Street journal* (new series) vol. 17 no. 4 December 1967 pp. 219-221. Jack wasn't anyone in the Holmes canon and Sherlock didn't catch him, so there.

Dibdin, Michael *The last Sherlock Holmes story* Cape (London) 1978. Holmes finishes the Ripper and Moriarty at a stroke.

Ellison, Harlan (editor) *Dangerous visions. Volume one* 359 p. Doubleday (New York) 1967; David Bruce and Watson (London) 1970.

Ellison, Harlan *The prowler in the city at the edge of the world* in *Dangerous visions*. Sequel to Bloch's *A toy for Juliette*.

Erskine, Margaret *Give up the ghost* 239 p. Hammond (London) 1949. A borderline case of a strangler preying on old ladies.

Farmer, Philip José *A feast unknown* 286p. Essex House (New York) 1969; Quartet (London) 1975. The son of Jack!

Farmer, Philip José *Lord of the trees* 183p. Severn House (London) 1982. Passing reference (p.43) to Lord Grandreth who drank the elixir of life and became the Ripper.

Fisher, Charles *A challenge from Baker Street* in *Leaves from the copper beeches* Livingstone (Narberth, PA.) 1959 pp. 15-32. Jack = Horace Harker is caught by Holmes (and employed by Moriarty).

Forssell, Iars *Jack Uppskäraren och andra visor tryckta i ar* (Stockholm) 1966. The Ripper provides the theme for an anti-capitalist poem.

Gardner, John *The return of Moriarty* Weidenfeld and Nicolson (London) 1974. Druitt as the Ripper, disposed of through the good offices of Professor Moriarty!

Gordon, Richard *The private life of Jack the Ripper: a novel* 279p. Heinemann (London) 1980. Dr Bertie Randolph anaesthetizing his victims before performing 'surgery'. "It's a wonder nobody spotted chloroform in the bodies." (p.265) A thin story broken up with undigested gobbets of historical background information.

Gordon, Richard M. *A punishment to fit the crimes* in *The fiend in you* edited by Charles Beaumont 158 p. Ballantine (New York) 1962. The trial and sentence of Saucy Jackie.

Grady, Thomas F. *Two bits from Boston* in the *Baker Street journal Christmas annual* no. 5 1960 pp. 272-5. Holmes to the rescue.

Greer, Terence *Ripper* 1973. A musical staged at the Half Moon Theatre in East London featuring a series of Rippers.

Hagen, Orlean *Who done it? A guide to detective, mystery and suspense fiction* 834p. Bowker (New York) 1969. The most fruitful source of fictional Ripperana and other forms of criminal clef.

Hamilton, Patrick *Hangover Square: a story of darkest Earl's Court* 279 p. Random (New York) 1941; Constable (London) 1941. Said to be derived from the Whitechapel murders — but how?

Hatherley, Frank *The Jack the Ripper show and how they wrote it* (1973) A British musical (with music by Jeremy Barlow) in which the killer changes with each performance and remains the same.

Heine, Maurice *Regards sur l'enfer anthropoclassique* in *Minotaure* (Paris) No. 8, 1936 pp. 41-45. The Ripper, disguised as a vicar, in conversation with the Marquis de Sade and others.

Heldenbrand, Page *Another Bohemian scandal* in the *Baker Street journal* vol. 4 no. 1 January 1949 pp. 72-3. One of Sherlock's failures.

Holmes, H. H. *The stripper.* Short story originally published in 1945 in *Ellery*

Queen's mystery magazine and later collected in Ellery Queen's *Twentieth century detective stories* 288 p. World Pub. Co. (New York) 1948 and reprinted in Barnard. This story is recommended by Anthony Boucher in his preface to Barker; both Boucher and Holmes being pseudonyms of W. A. P. White! (The latter alias was shared by the murderer H. W. Mudgett). Concerns an eclectic disciple of the Ripper.

Hubin, Allen J. *The bibliography of crime fiction 1749 - 1975: listing all mystery, detective, suspense, police and gothic fiction in book form published in the English language* U. of California (San Diego) 1979. Ambitious!

Hummelman, Franz *see* Leonard, Ef.

Huru Jack Uppskäraren blev tillfangatagen (How Jack the Ripper was caught) Skandia (Stockholm) (c. 1900) No. 18 in a series called *Sherlock Holmes detective stories*. Thirty seven women killed by Dr Fitzgerald.

In the slaughteryard a chapter from *The adventures of the Adventurers' Club* (c. 1891) reprinted in Parry, Michel *Jack the knife* pp. 74-86. Jack boiled in a vat of vitriol.

Jack L'Eventreur strip cartoon in *Cauchemar* (Paris) (c. 1972) no. 6 pp. 23-44. A black magic theory is reported to Scotland Yard but rebutted — by the Ripper!

James, Stuart *Jack the Ripper: based on the original screen play by Jimmy Sangster, plus a true-to-life account of the actual Ripper murders ... by Bill Doll* 157 p. Monarch (Connecticut); Fell (New York) 1960. Salacious drivel. Sir David Rogers hunting Mary Clarke. Ten picayune pages on the real murders.

Jones, Elwyn and Lloyd, John *see* FACTS AND THEORIES; MUSIC AND FILMS etc. (under *Jack the Ripper*).

Kennedy, Bruce *Jack in the abyss* in the *Baker Street journal* (new series) vol. 17 no. 4 December 1967 p. 222. Moriarty.

Kersh, Gerald *Poppy's ballad of Marty Tabram* in *The angel and the cuckoo* 342 p. Heinemann (London) 1967. A merry ditty of twenty verses included in this novel reveals that "He was a surgeon in disguise, the greatest in the nation".

La Cour, Tage and Mogensen, Harald *The murder book: an illustrated history of the detective story* 192p. Allen and Unwin 1971. Has two pages on Ripper fiction.

Laing, Allan MacDonald *Jack the Ripper* in *Bank Holiday on Parnassus* 145 p. Allen and Unwin (London) 1941. A four line poem surveys Jack's childhood.

Lauterbach, Edward S. *Holmes and the Ripper* in the *Baker Street journal* (new series) vol. 18 no. 2 June 1968 pp. 111-3. Thirty one stanzas of doggerel describe Moriarty being caught by Holmes and Watson.

Lauterbach, Edward S. *Jack the R.I.P.* in the *Pontine dossier annual* no. 2 1971 pp. 79-80. An unpleasant Jack portrayed in verse for the Praed Street Irregulars (Holmes-freaks).

Law, John *In darkest London* (London) 1889. Deathbed confession of the Ripper as a slaughter-house worker.

Leavitt, Jack *Mr Holmes please take the Strand* in the *Baker Street journal* (new series) vol. 18 no. 3 September 1968 pp. 170-9. Under cross-examination Holmes admits to being the Ripper.

Lee, Manfred B *see* Queen, Ellery

Leonard, Ef *Het Kcaj-raport* in *In spin-opnieuw gaat de bocht in*. The Ripper as an alien from Dramur studying female sex-organs using the body of a human named Throckmorton. More details please! (Information supplied by Michel Parry)

Lovesey, Peter *Swing, swing together* 190p. MacMillan (London) 1976. A former Ripper suspect is suspected of two further murders — or was he the intended victim? Good period flavour.

Lowndes, Marie Belloc *The lodger* Scribner (New York) 1911; Methuen (London) 1913 and many editions since. A best-selling novel which first appeared as a short story in *McClure's magazine* January 1911 pp. 262-77 and was reprinted by Barnard in that form. "Sold something like half a million at sixpence in the Reader's Library" (Lowndes). Inspired two plays and several films. See also MUSIC AND FILMS: *The lodger, The man in the attic, The phantom fiend*.

Lustgarten, Edgar Marcus *A case to answer* 203 p. Eyre and Spottiswoode (London) 1947. This tale about a disciple of the Ripper embarking on his crusade was published in America as *One more unfortunate*.

MacDonald, Philip *Mystery of the dead police* Doubleday (New York) 1933. Barnard lists it as Ripper-derived.

Marsh, Ngaio *Singing in the shrouds* 225 p. Little (Boston, USA) 1958; Collins (London) 1959. A revamped Ripper on the high seas.

Morland, Nigel *Death for sale* 192 p. Hale (London) 1957. Tenuous link with Whitechapel killings.

Neitzke, Gordon *Sherlock Holmes and Jack the Ripper* in Williamson, J.N. and Williams, H.B. (editors) *Illustrious clients' third casebook* The Illustrious Clients (Indianapolis) 1953 pp. 80-3. Finding the Ripper is elementary for dear Watson.

Nisbet, Hume *The demon spell* 1894. Reprinted in Parry, Michel *Jack the knife* pp. 40-5. The Ripper ripped.

Norton, Graham *Was Gladstone Jack the Ripper?* in *Queen* (London) September 1970 pp. 52-3. Of course he was.

Oliver, N. T. *Jack the Ripper* Donohne (USA) (c. 1911). May be another edition of the next item. Otherwise untraced although listed in the *U S catalogue* for 1912.

Oliver, N. T. *The Whitechapel mystery: Jack the Ripper, a psychological problem* 225 p. Continental Pub. Co. (Chicago) 1891. Number 8 of the bi-weekly *Patrol detective series* according to the title page. John Dewey a New York policeman tracks down Dr. Westinghouse (the Ripper) in London and becomes his accomplice! The Library of Congress catalogue lists a book of the same title published by the Eagle Pub. Co. (Chicago) 1889 under E. O. Tilburn, Oliver's real name.

Parry, Michel (editor) *Jack the knife: tales of Jack the Ripper* 160p. Mayflower (London) 1975. Anthology of Ripper fiction.

Parry, Michel (editor) *The reign of terror: great Victorian horror stories* Sphere (London) 1973. Includes two Ripper stories.

Pember, Ron and de Marne, Denis *Jack the Ripper: a musical play* 53p. French (London) 1976. Play with music by Pember first presented at the Ambassador's Theatre, London on September 17th 1974. Montague Druitt as the villain (and magician).

Pinkerton, A. Frank *The Whitechapel murders: or an American detective in London* Laird (New York) 1889. Listed by Hubin.

Pumilia, Joseph *Forever stand the stones* in Parry, Michel *Jack the knife* pp. 21-39. Wygiff the Druid does his thing. The Ripper notes were badly written because that skill doesn't come naturally to 2000 year old Celts.

Queen, Ellery *The misadventures of Sherlock Holmes* Little, Brown (Boston) (1944) A suppressed anthology which included Boucher's *Jack el Distripador*.

Queen, Ellery *Nick the knife*. A radio play referred to by Boucher. Frederic Dannay does not recall it.

Queen, Ellery *Sherlock Holmes versus Jack The Ripper* 271 p. Gollancz (London) 1967. Published in USA as *A study in terror* Lancer (New York) 1966. Inspired by a film of that title. The Duke did it!

Reade, Leslie *The stranger*. A three act play staged at the Playhouse, New York for sixteen performances from February 12th 1945. "A travelling cobbler is chief suspect and, as it turns out, likewise chief innocent".

Reid, Hugh *Dulcie* in the *Fourth Pan book of horror stories* 271 p. Pan (London) 1963. The murderer collects heads for his mantelpiece.

Rogers, Kay *Love story* in *Magazine of fantasy and science fiction* (New York) 1951, reprinted in Barnard. The heroine is a Ripper victim.

Russell, Ray *Unholy trinity* 141 p. Bantam (New York) 1967; Sphere (London) 1971. *Sagittarius* the third novella of the trilogy proceeds via Stevenson's Mr. Hyde/Jack the Ripper, through a reincarnation or disciple of Bluebeard ...

Salowich, Alex N. *He could not have sat idly* in the *Baker Street journal* (new series) vol. 18 no. 2 June 1968 pp. 107-9. Jack as Sir James Saunders. Holmes kept quiet to protect the eminent.

Sandoe, James *Criminal clef: tales and plays based on real crimes* in *Wilson library bulletin* (New York) December 1946 pp. 299-307. Includes four Ripper tales.

Sansom, William *The intruder* in *Cosmopolitan magazine* (New York) 1948, reprinted in Barnard. A strangler at large in Victoria.

Shew, Edward Spencer *Hands of the Ripper* 160 p. Sphere (London) 1971. Written "in conjunction with the Hammer films production" the plot is so far out that it's on the way back.

Skene, Anthony *The Ripper returns* Pemberton (Manchester) 1948. He does, in time to be detected by Sexton Blake. Recorded by Hubin.

Sladek, John *Black aura* 224p. Cape (London) 1974. Pages 59-60 offer as convincing a case against Dr Watson as most of the official candidates can muster.

Smith, Edgar W. *The suppressed adventures of the worst man in London* in *Baker Street and beyond: together with semi-trifling monographs* The Baker Street Irregulars (Moristown, NJ) 1957. The maestro may have helped catch the Ripper.

Stevens, R.L. *The legacy* in *Ellery Queen's mystery magazine* August 1972 pp. 121-5. A hereditary killer.

Stevens, Shane *By reason of insanity* Weidenfeld and Nicolson (London) 1979. Thomas Bishop pursues a Ripper-style career in modern America. Or does he?

Tapper, Oscar *Jack the Knife* Elam (London) 18 p. 2nd edition 1970. Verse drama first published in *East London arts magazine* autumn 1964 and performed April 1965.

Vachell, Horace Annesley *The lodger*. Play produced at Maxine Elliott Theatre, New York from January 8th 1917 for 56 performances. Adapted from the Lowndes novel and starring Lionel Atwill as the innocent lodger.

Veheyne, C. *Horror* 160p. Brown, Watson (London) 1962. The Ripper is a frustrated clergyman encouraged by his Mum.

Wedekind, Frank *Der Erdgeist* 1895 and *Die Büchse der Pandora* 1904. Two plays by the German dramatist translated as *Earth spirit* 1914 and *Pandora's box* 1918, both published in New York. New translation by Stephen/Spender, Vision (London) 1952. The heroine is murdered by the Ripper. See also MUSIC AND FILMS.

Walsh, Ray *The Mycroft memoranda* 186 p. Deutsch (London) 1984. Holmes seeks his man, again.

Wilson, Colin *Ritual in the dark* 416 p. Gollancz (London); Houghton (Boston, USA) 1960. Ripper in a contemporary setting.

Zola, Emile *La bête humaine* 1890. Colin Wilson suggests (in his *Criminal history of mankind*) that this novel was inspired by the Ripper's activities.

5   MUSIC AND FILMS, ETC.

The lodger by Marie Belloc Lowndes has inspired a number of film interpretations and several other Ripper variants have been traced including two operas. Other films, songs, television and radio programmes must have been produced and I should like to hear about them.

The works in this section have been listed under title.

The Avengers see *Fog.*

Brecht, Bertolt see FICTION AND DRAMA

The case of the unmentioned case see FICTION AND DRAMA: Bailey, L.W.

Champagne gallop 1973. Swedish pornographic (?) comedy film starring Martin Ljung as the Ripper; directed by Vernon P Becker.

Dr Jekyll and Sister Hyde 1972. Hammer film written by Brian Clemens and directed by Roy Ward Baker. Martine Beswick does her thing.

Farson's guide to the British Associated Rediffusion TV programmes (London) 5th and 12th November 1959. Dan Farson interviewed various survivors of the period who told apocryphal stories. Revealed initials (MJD) of MacNaghten's suspect.

Fog British film in the *Avengers* series shown on ITV with Nigel Green as the President of the Jack the Ripper Club.

Format Westward television programme of April 10th 1972 featured an interview of Michael Harrison and Daniel Farson by Colin Wilson.

Hands of the Ripper 1971. Directed by Peter Sasdy for Hammer Productions (London), starring Eric Porter; screenplay by L. W. Davidson based on story by Edward Spencer Shew. A splendid example of the genre. Jack adopts the perfect disguise but don't kiss Angharad Rees — it could be fatal!

Hangover Square 1945. Film of the novel (q.v.) directed by John Brahm for Fox.

The horror of Hawk Street shown on BBC 1 on July 7th 1972.

Jack the Ripper 1958. Mid Century film (distributed by Regal films) featuring Lee Paterson and directed by Robert S. Baker. The screen-play by Jimmy Sangster was based on a story by Peter Hammond and Colin Craig. A "shoddy horror feature" (*New York times*). See FICTION AND DRAMA: James, Stuart.

Jack the Ripper 1973. BBC Television dramatization in six parts (July 13th-August 17th 1973) has Detective Chief Superintendants Barlow and Watt in pursuit of the Ripper after having given him 85 years start. Introduces the Freemason theory and attempts to link the Cleveland Street Scandal with the painter Sickert and the murders. See FACTS AND THEORIES: Jones, Elwyn and Lloyd, John.

Der Januskopf 1920. Screenplay by Hans Janowitz, based on *Dr. Jekyll and Mr. Hyde*, directed by F. W. Murnau. German.

Late night line-up July 28th 1972 on BBC Television. Daniel Farson, Michael Harrison, Donald Rumbelow and Colin Wilson discussed Harrison's theory. The conversation was reported in the *Listener* for August 17th under the heading *Relatively ripping*.

The lodger 1932. Olympic film directed by Maurice Elvey, based on the book by Marie Belloc Lowndes.

The lodger 1944. Starring Merle Oberon and George Sanders, directed by John Brahm for Fox. Notable for anachronistic use of fingerprints. Laird Cregar is the Ripper.

The lodger British TV film with Charles Gray as the Ripper. Further details please.

The lodger 1960. Opera in two acts by Phyllis Tate, first performed in 1960 and televised in 1964.

The lodger: a story of the London fog 1926. Silent film directed by Alfred Hitchcock for Gainsborough (Piccadilly Pictures) and starring Ivor Novello. Adapted by Hitchcock and Eliot Stannard from the Lowndes novel.

London black-out murders 1942. American film, with screenplay by Curt Siodmak, directed by George Sherman. (listed in Barnard q.v.)

Loulou 1923. Condensed and watered-down version of the Wedekind plays and devoid of the Ripper sequences later re-introduced in *Pandora's box (Lulu)*. Asta Nielsen is Lulu.

Lulu, premier 1937, unfinished. An opera in three acts based on two plays by Wedekind. The heroine meets her fate at the hands of the Ripper. Record released by Columbia in 1952. Composed by Alban Berg.

Lured 1947. American film by Leo Rosten and directed by Douglas Sirk with George Sanders and Boris Karloff. Concerns a homicidal maniac preying on girls and Barnard records it as based on the Ripper theme.

The man in the attic 1953. Fox film loosely based on *The lodger* by Lowndes. Directed by Hugo Fregonese with Jack Palance as Jack.

Mary Clarke A track on the Black Widow LP called *Black Widow*. Music published by April Music/Magus Music. CBS 64133.

Masque (Leicester) no. 4 May 1971. Duplicated film magazine devotes an issue to Sherlock Holmes, Ripper and 'gaslight' films.

Murder by decree 1980. English film by John Hopkins, directed by Bob Clark and based on the Sickert story. Christopher Plummer is Sherlock Holmes, James Mason is Watson. Highlight Theatrical Productions.

Nick the knife see FICTION AND DRAMA: Queen, Ellery

The night stalker. Episode in the American *Kolchak* series broadcast on Central Television on 15th October 1983. Crime reporter Carl Kolchak shocks a prolific and long-lived Ripper whose only fear is electricity.

No orchids for Lulu 1967. Austrian film based on the Wedekind plays with Mario Adorf as the Ripper. DUK Films.

Pandora's box (Lulu) 1922. Film directed by G. W. Pabst based on the Wedekind plays and starring Louise Brooks as Lulu with Gustav Diessl as the Ripper. Nero films A. G. Screenplay published as:

Pabst, G. W. *Pandora's Box (Lulu): a film. Classic film scripts series* Lorrimer (London) 1971.

The phantom fiend American title of *The lodger* 1932.

The phantom raspberry blower of old London town in *The two Ronnies* on BBC 1 September-October 1976. Written by Spike Milligan and 'a gentleman' for Ronnies Barker and Corbett.

Room to let 1949. English film by John Gilling and Godfrey Grayson (director) based on a radio play by Margery Allingham.

The ruling class 1972. Film of the play (q.v.) starring Peter O'Toole and directed by Peter Medak for Keep Films Ltd.

Screaming Mimi 1957. Based on the novel by Fredric Brown.

Smiler with a knife. A documentary programme about the murders broadcast by BBC Radio on April 12th 1967. Written by Tony Van den Bergh.

Study in terror 1965. Based on a story by Donald and Derek Ford and starring John Neville as Holmes. Directed by James Hill. Georgia Brown's singing makes it all worthwhile.

Till death us do part BBC Television, November 19th 1975. Johnny Speight's popular comedy series has a reference to the Ripper as "the Jew Gladstone" who became Prime Minister to evade suspicion. Queen Victoria found him out and retired to Windsor Castle to avoid his clutches!

Time after time 1979. Malcolm McDowell as H. G. Wells goes travelling with David Warner as Jack. Directed and written by Nicholas Meyer; based on a story by Karl Alexander and Steve Hayes.

24 hours (BBC Television) Programmes have included Professor Camps interviewed on April 15th 1966; Thomas Stowell interviewed by Kenneth Allsop on November 2nd 1970; and an item following Stowell's death, broadcast on November 16th 1970.

The waxworks (*Das Wachsfigurenkabinett*) 1924. Film directed by Paul Leni with Werner Krauss as the Ripper in the third episode of a screenplay by Henrik Galeen. Neptun Films (Germany).

Who was Jack the Ripper? BBC Radio programme in the *Other Victorians* series broadcast on June 1st 1972. Written by Michell Raper; the text was later (1974) published by the Tabaret Press.

Wolf from the fold an episode in the space-saga *Star trek* broadcast on BBC Television on May 3rd 1972. Enter an entity which breeds on terror (alias Jack the Ripper) then exit by blasting into deep space. Originally broadcast as episode 42 in the USA (1967). Script by Robert Bloch.

Yours truly, Jack the Ripper American TV film with screenplay by Robert Bloch, based on his own story.

ACKNOWLEDGEMENTS

My thanks are offered to Ian Bradley, Tom Cullen, Daniel Farson, Alida Flynn, Joe Gaute, Otto Holm, Roger Johnson, Klas Lithner, Donald McCormick, Tom McDade, George MacLennan, Nigel Morland, Robin Odell, Michel Parry, Margaride Pino, Michelle Raccagni, Sue Taylor, Charles Toase, Colin Wilson and Tom Wilson for help and advice.

Various libraries have proved invaluable including those of the Bodleian, British Museum, Commissioner's Reference Library (New Scotland Yard), London Boroughs of Merton and Tower Hamlets and in America the Library of Congress and New York Public Library.

3 NAME AND SUBJECT INDEX

"Blessed are the drowsy men: for they shall soon drop off."
                    (Nietzsche *Thus spake Zarathustra*)

NAME TITLE AND SUBJECT
INDEX